LIFE *according* TO JAG

LIFE *according* TO JAG

Simple Truths and Lessons Learned

KATHRYN VALENTINE

iUniverse LLC
Bloomington

Life according to Jag
Simple Truths and Lessons Learned

Heart Centered Publishing 461 Hudson Lane Victor MT. 59875
Editor: Angela Breidenbach

The persons and events portrayed in this work are as experienced by the author. Some names have been changed for privacy and protection.

iUniverse books may be ordered through booksellers or by contacting:

iUniverse LLC
1663 Liberty Drive
Bloomington, IN 47403
www.iuniverse.com
1-800-Authors (1-800-288-4677)

ISBN: 978-1-4759-9902-0 (sc)
ISBN: 978-1-4759-9901-3 (hc)
ISBN: 978-1-4759-9900-6 (ebk)

Library of Congress Control Number: 2013912925

Printed in the United States of America

iUniverse rev. date: 08/12/2013

This book is dedicated to my husband,
Bill Patenaude, ever patient, kind and gentle.
Thank you for believing in me.

CONTENTS

Acknowledgment

Cherished are memories of my family. Strong, independent, warm women raised me. My mother was my best friend and mentor. Her sister Margaret guided me in life's wisdom. My grandmother, Blanche Peltier, was filled with affection, adventure, and a pure love of life.

All three of these precious women are no longer with me but I could hear them cheer me on as I wrote this book. All three are a part of the wisdom, creativity, and passion you'll read about in the following pages. They never doubted this book would come to pass.

These women have blessed me and they continue to live on through me. So I want to say thank you to my wonderful family.

Kathryn Marie Patenaude December 2012

INTRODUCTION

This book is about the power of words and the splendor of not just knowing what a specific word means, but what can happen when you take ownership of that word and tell your own story.

Stories are the substance to the words. In addition to writing about the power of words, I've shared short stories that capture the essence of each word and the influence it's played in my life.

Who am I? I'm a professional horseman. I've owned and shown horses in the American Quarter Horse Association, American Paint Horse Association, and the National Reining Horse Association. I've had the incredible experience of working and learning from some of the best trainers in the industry such as John Lyons, Shawn Flarida, and Sandy Strain to name a few. I've been a featured speaker at Equine Affaire and many other wonderful horse expositions across the country.

The incredible part, for me, is my story doesn't end there. I've also used my talents and skills to reach those outside the horse world. I love teaching leadership skills to an array of large and small business and associations. Being able to go beyond the equine world is a rewarding experience. Much of my life has been filled with the wonders of working with a wide array of horses and their owners. My own horse, Jag, for which this book is titled, played a huge part in who I became and how I see the world around me. Time with Jag helped me grow as a horseman and as a person. Jag allowed me to experience life in ways I'd never before imagined.

I owe so much to this wonderful animal with all his patience, kindness, and wisdom.

Words are funny. They can trigger different emotions for all of us. For instance, the word *perseverance* bothers me. It makes me feel self-righteous. I'm not sure why. I mention this because I wonder what words you will connect with and which words will leave you feeling unattached. As you read this book, be aware of how the topic word in each chapter makes you feel. Remember any word can be described by its definition, but a word only becomes powerful when we feel it. The emotion we attach to the word makes it real.

When I came up with the idea for this book, I chose to write because I believe words are powerful when given emotion. Words alone are simply—words. But my idea would take words we all know and use them to write stories of myself, Jag, family, friends, and even rivals to give the words I've chosen emotion, creating significance.

I hope to inspire you to create significance through your stories. We all have a book inside us. Everyone has a story. I hope through my life lessons, you'll reflect on yourself, your life, and those who touched your life along the journey.

I'm an average person with my share of trials. I'm human. I don't always have a perfect attitude; I can get pretty down on myself at times. But I choose to believe my life has purpose and it's my responsibility to grow and share the journey with others so our lives have meaning.

Each day is an opportunity. We can choose to stay where we are or we can choose to move forward to grow to grasp our hopes and dreams. My wish is you'll reach and grow and believe! I hope you'll find these words as powerful as I do, and you'll reflect on your own life stories. May you enjoy that journey as much as you enjoy this book!

CHAPTER 1

ADAPTABILITY

As a student, I worked with some top equestrian trainers on the East Coast. Bill and Sandy Strain were known for outstanding youth programs. I was privileged to work with them for several show seasons. One particular rider exercise, they called the Echo, was mentally and physically exhausting. Although the Echo was a great and effective drill, we students dreaded it. But we always knew it was coming.

The drill was unpredictable. Sandy would call out different maneuvers, sometimes at lightning speed, and expect her students to stay mentally focused and strong. Often a loose dog or pig (*yes, I said pig*) ran through our patterns or she might have a helper get in the way by singing a tune, flapping a tarp, or pushing a baby stroller to see if the rider could stay on track and avoid distraction. We never knew what disturbance Sandy would come up with or how a horse might respond. The Echo taught us to be mentally strong, how to stay in the moment, and show our horses at their best no matter what might happen.

Years later I had the opportunity to be an assistant coach at a youth barn on the East Coast at a private facility. A great opportunity to begin my teaching career! Each week this private facility would invite Sandy Strain run a workshop for the young men and woman to prepare for the AQHA Congress in Columbus, Ohio.

I was excited to be a part of this great facility and again work with Sandy, not as a student, but as her assistant coach. After a few workshops I realized she never asked these students to do the Echo. Was she waiting for the right timing?

After a few weeks I asked Sandy why she hadn't used the Echo drill with this group. I reminded her as a student, we did that exercise daily, without fail.

I remember the warmth and sincerity in Sandy's voice as she said, "Kathy, there is a big difference between the group of students you've worked with and these students. You must learn to adapt to what each individual horse rider team needs. Every rider and horse is different. Learn about their personality and learning styles. Although the end result is a winning team, to get there you may have to use different strategies to bring out their best ride."

I've learned a lot from some great coaches, from Sandy Strain to John Lyons to Shawn Flarida. They taught me about passion, commitment, persistence, and intensity. But I also learned adaptability.

Here I am, thirty years later, offering an annual apprenticeship program in Victor, Montana, and around the country. Each year I change the program just enough . . . just enough to be sure I serve my students well and adapt new ways to communicate for the best learning experience I can create.

A student instructor once asked, "Kathy you didn't teach this exercise the same last year?"

With a smile on my face, and some years of teaching and learning under my belt, I explain to my student why I do what I do. Hopefully this is my time to pass on the very same gift handed down to me.

In teaching, remember no individual or group is the same as you taught the day before, the year before, or the decade before. Your plan has to suit who you and your students are right now. You must always be willing to change and adapt. When you do, success begins to grow for both you and your students.

Let's take this one step further by thinking about adaptability in everyday life. Learning to let go of things that no longer serve you mentally, emotionally, and physically then replacing them with something wonderful and productive can be life changing. Having adaptability present in our day-to-day lives is certainly worth considering.

CHAPTER 2

ADVERSITY

I believe what makes a great rider, and a great individual, is the manner in which they handle adversity. When faced with a tough moment, do you keep moving forward, looking ahead at a positive outcome, or do you let it beat you?

Adversity can help you grow and offers life lessons far more valuable than any success. You learn to overcome an obstacle and grow as a person. It's an opportunity to grow and learn about character and strength in the horse world and in life.

In the late 1990s, I was searching for a business partner who had integrity and a passion to make a difference in the horse world. I met Ron in Parachute, Colorado. I knew immediately he was a man of character and integrity. I did not yet know he was also a man with true grit.

Ron decided he wanted to buy a horse to show in Western Trail. He set a goal to buy a green broke horse and train it, promote it, and qualify it for the AQHA World Show. After countless trips looking at horses all over the country, he found a three-year-old filly up in Canada. She had no impressive pedigree, and no show record, but something about her wouldn't let him walk away.

He paid a good amount of money for this filly and was excited to get her home to begin his dream. Soon after he purchased this horse, she became very ill. Vet after vet looked at her with no answers. She grew sick and weak. The vets described a rare form of leukemia. The original prognosis—bleak. Months passed, as did the entire show season. Ron went to the barn several times a day and hand-walked his horse, groomed her daily and spent time with her. He never lost faith she would somehow recover.

The weeks turned into months, and at a time when many would have cut their losses, Ron continued believing and working toward his dream. He decided if he couldn't ride, he could build a wonderful foundation of trust and communication on the ground. Little by little, the filly took a turn for the better. She put on weight, her coat shone. Soon he could put some light rides on her and so began their journey. Now a five-year-old, she'd lost a ton of show time over the past year.

However, Ron kept moving forward with his plan. He kept his faith. When others told him it was too late to qualify the filly for the world competition, he kept pressing forward.

Fancy not only qualified for the AQHA World Show Event but she won Junior Western Trail and was tenth in the world in Western Riding. What an incredible journey for both of them!

The adversity did not beat him. Ron saw it as an opportunity to grow as a person and horseman. How blessed I'm to have known and worked with this man. His strong and courageous belief in himself and his horse carried him through. He saw a destination beyond the devastation.

What a great lesson for all of us who face adversity in our lives. We must keep the faith and believe in ourselves. Learn to see past the problem to the opportunity. Failure can never be your final destination. Let it be a way to grow as a person and teach you to move forward in your riding and in your life.

CHAPTER 3

ATTITUDE

Attitude is described in Webster's Dictionary as, "an opinion or general feeling about something, a positive attitude to change."

Even the dictionary uses "positive" to describe this word. We all know someone can have a negative attitude. The words positive or negative are only important when we attach emotion.

Attitude is about choice. We can choose how to feel or how to deal with a variety of situations. Our thoughts are powerful and it's not always easy choosing to be positive during a difficult situation. It's the emotion we attach that determines the outcome.

I grew up in a broken home. My dad was an alcoholic and my mom spent most of her time trying to protect us kids. She chose to divorce so we could be safe and have a chance of a better life. I stop and reflect on what "a chance at a better life" really means. To me the chance meant a new home in a new area, a different school, and new friends but I was still the same young girl who grew up in an abusive home with a self-centered alcoholic father.

Was I really starting over? I don't think so. I had to dig deep for a good attitude so I could grow and learn from the world around me. As I write this I realize even in the turmoil of an abusive home I was, for the most part, a loving and happy child. Don't get me wrong, there were plenty of nights I cried myself to sleep or ran to my neighbors to call the police sure my dad would kill my mom.

Mom, through all of this, held her head high. As she struggled to figure out how to move forward she stayed strong and loving to her children. Mom always put herself between her kids and my dad. I never was blessed with children but my maternal instinct is alive and well when it comes to my animals. I wonder if that's why I protect my horses and dogs with my life.

Too often we are victims of our circumstance. We feel wounded and trapped from our past, making it difficult to move forward and to grow. Yes, attitude is everything. I could have played the part of a victim. I chose the attitude that I'm a worthy and valuable person who deserves to be happy and fulfilled.

Often times when I'm working with horses I hear clients say, "That horse will never be worth a dime!" or "Why bother trying to train that worthless animal?" Now if I believe this nonsense, then the horse I train would have no chance to grow and learn. I would have sealed his fate. Instead, I'm careful to adopt the attitude that all creatures, big and small, have value and worth. It's my responsibility to nurture and develop a positive attitude in my students and my horses.

The reason I'm able to have such a positive attitude is my mom, grandmother, and aunt all taught me about having faith and believing in myself. I watched my mom struggle to free herself from an abusive relationship. She was a strong and confident woman filled with passion and goodness. What a role model for a young woman to have!

I believe the lessons Mom taught me as a young woman contribute to who I am today as a friend, spouse, sister, aunt, and also my profession as a horse trainer. I understand attitude is about choice and we all have the option to choose our destination.

My hope for you, dear reader, is that if you struggle with having a positive outlook, take the time to find people who can help nurture and guide you to change. You'll begin to reap the rewards of being positive. Keep in mind we always teach and influence others. It's a gift to offer others the chance to learn about a good attitude.

Part of the reason I'm writing this book is not only to share with you my story, but to inspire you to write stories and share your journey with others. If you have a good attitude and are a positive, upbeat person take the time to reflect. Consider those that may have helped you gain these wonderful attributes. I bet you have a great story others would love to hear.

CHAPTER 4

BALANCE

Motivation, drive, passion, and success: just reading these words can send a spark of enthusiasm to our hearts. We all know these traits are key to a successful career and life. However, the ability to balance our lives in all areas from work to family to hobbies, religion, friendships, and everything in-between are just as important.

I was reminded of the need for balance when Jag was a five-year-old and we were worked hard traveling for clinics and demonstrations. We traveled over 20,000 miles that year. We both looked tired from the stress.

Jag never complains. He doesn't get grumpy when he is pushed to his limits. He simply cowboys up and gets the job done. In Jag's four-year-old year I was asked to travel across the U.S. and give demonstrations and clinics. I'm sorry my enthusiasm clouded my ability to see the toll this took on Jag.

We were in Parachute, Colorado, doing a "Trainers Only Clinic." I'm competitive and wanted to be seen as one of the best trainers there. We were working on *haunches in* that day (a very difficult maneuver physically for a horse to hold over a period of time). I was determined to nail it, at all gaits. Jag bless his big, old heart gave 110%, as usual. It was a long day and we had accomplished a lot. We were both tired. As I put Jag in his stall, he just didn't seem right. Anyone who owns a horse knows what that means. For those who don't, it's an intuitive sense, unspoken yet there's a clear message. It comes from learning how to still one's mind and deeply connect with another. If you are a parent you've witnessed this same phenomenon with your children.

Jag was quiet and began to eat. I felt restlessness within and decided to keep a close watch. Later that evening Jag began to show signs of colic. Panicked, I called the vet and waited for him to arrive. Jag nuzzled me. My beautiful big paint taught me a lesson about what is important in life. Although he never complained, even miserable with a bellyache, Jag's nuzzle told me its okay, we can get through this.

We did make it through that day, but I learned an important lesson—balancing one's life. I became so engrossed in my career I lost sight of the bigger picture. I had very little contact with my family or friends. Jag was being worked hard and had no time to simply be a horse. I was tired and obviously not always making the best decisions. How precious and fragile life can be. I made a promise that night to Jag, and to myself, to be more balanced in our lives.

Jag recovered from his colic and the next day we were asked to stay on and teach at this trainers' event because we had done such an outstanding job. I declined the offer and loaded Jag up for the ride to the East Coast. I've never regretted that decision or the many others I made to balance my life and Jag's in a much better way.

Jag and I still enjoy doing demonstrations and clinics. However, we also take time to enjoy hitting the trails or hanging out in the pasture, Jag grazing contently and I reading a good book. I love and honor my family and friends by spending time with them and nurturing our relationships.

Whatever your role, from CEO to a stay-at-home entrepreneur, balance your life. Listen to those around you and hear your inner voice. Slow down and regroup. Make whatever changes to ensure you have balance in your life. Balance puts things in perspective; it brings joy and peace. Balance keeps track of the things we hold near and dear to our hearts.

CHAPTER 5

BELIEF

As a child I learned how magical the words, "I love you", can be. However, I also learned how powerful it's to have someone say, "I believe in you." This simple little phrase can mean the difference between the fear of failure or the courage to try. When you look someone in the eye and say, "I believe in you", the subscript says, "You will not be alone in this journey because I support and believe in you."

When someone else believes, it helps us overcome anxiety when we are alone. Belief raises confidence level and gives the strength to try new things—even what may have seemed impossible alone. My definition of confidence is a belief in oneself.

When someone believes in and supports your idea or venture that support makes setbacks easier and can turn a negative into a positive. Sharing in a mistake builds confidence as much as sharing in a victory.

Belief does not come naturally. You have to earn and deserve it. Belief in someone or something is trust. Relationships with people as well as horses need trust. If I lie and violate the relationship, it becomes more difficult for you to believe what I say. If you've built a relationship with your horse, then you do something that causes him to become frightened or injured, he'll struggle trusting the next time you interact. So belief is a powerful gift that you can give to someone, but it's also fragile.

When I think about belief, the first person who comes to mind is my mother. Mom was the strongest and gentlest person I have ever known. She loved me because she was my mom but she believed in me because she could see beyond the here and now. She was a woman with vision. What a gift to give to a daughter—the gift to believe.

At seventeen, I told Mom I wanted to own a trucking company and drive long haul across the country. Now, my mother was a nurse and had great hope I would also go into the medical field. Imagine her thoughts as I announced my new venture of long-haul truck driver! But she sat down with me and said, "You can do, and be, anything you want to be. I believe in you and you will be successful."

And I was. When I decided to change careers fifteen years later, it was no surprise Mom would cheer me on once again. Go back to when I told my mother I wanted to be a long-haul truck driver. What if she'd said, "Oh my gosh Kathy, what are you thinking? Are you crazy? That's no life for a young woman—you'll never make it." Wow, how different my life may have been!

My mother instilled such wonderful gifts in me; honesty, integrity, commitment, and belief in myself. I always knew she cheered me on and stayed close by if I fell and needed a hand up.

I'm always honored to help my students achieve their dreams. I remember the courage and strength I've experienced when someone believed in me. My hope is to pass down that same gift to others.

I'd like to share a slightly different story that involves Jag and the importance of our attitude and convictions. I bought Jag as a three-year-old from a horse dealer. Jag had gone through four sale barns and finally landed in Hartford, Connecticut. Everyone (except my mom) thought I was crazy. "He keeps being sold for a reason Kathy, he'll never make a good all around horse for you." I called his previous owners and everyone gave a similar response. "He's pushy and hardheaded. He can be aggressive. Jag was bred to be a halter horse, and he is pretty. Pretty doesn't necessarily mean he has brains."

When I looked at Jag that day at the sale barn, I saw a beautiful creature whose presence spoke to my heart. I was taught to follow my heart and to believe. As I wrote out a check for my new horse, I stood next to him and thought, "I believe in you my friend. I will give you every chance I can to prove everyone wrong."

And prove himself he has. From dressage to western pleasure, western trail, cow work, ranch work, drill team, and lesson horse clinic/demo horse, and more, Jag is the best horse I may ever own. Jag has been by my side for fourteen years. He continues to win the heart of audiences everywhere we go.

I had some knowledge of what I wanted, a little faith, and a lot of heart and belief that Jag would be a wonderful equine partner.

So, what are you waiting for? Even if you've never had the gift of someone believing in you, you can take the first step in believing in yourself. Then you can give that gift away by believing in someone else. What a great tradition and life lesson to pass on to others.

CHAPTER 6

CARING

Compassion is genuine concern for a person or an animal. Compassion is displayed in the good times as well as the bad.

It's important to be a caring and compassionate person both in my business and personal life. When you show compassion, you build trust and from there all things are possible. Caring can also build confidence. With unconditional support, you gain confidence in yourself and in the other person.

Compassion is developed by nurturing individual relationships; caring when you have nothing to gain or lose. You show compassion because it's the right thing to do. I've worked hard building relationships based on honesty, trust, and respect. I care about those around me and I'm not afraid to go out on a limb for someone I care about. I have often helped friends and colleagues and never expect anything in return. In fact, it's very hard for me to ask for help in any way.

CARING IN ACTION

I bought a beautiful APHA mare in 2004. She had quite a history of aggressiveness and had proven dangerous to her owner. I decided to take Lacee on as a project. The owner felt she was worth $4,500, and after some negotiating, we settled on $3,500. A lot of money for a four-year-old mare no one could handle! Imagine the amount of criticism I received for this decision. Not many employees or clients liked this mare. I even had one employee threaten to quit if I kept her. My response? "Don't let the door hit you on the way out."

So my journey began. For almost two years I re-schooled this mare. She turned out to be one of the nicest, most talented horses I've ever owned. She won my heart. I can honestly say she taught me more than any horse I've ever owned.

Less than three years after I purchased Lacee, she was diagnosed with navicular disease. I was crushed. I had three vets x-ray her thinking there must be a mistake. I tried all the different options from drugs to corrective shoeing. As the months went by, Lacee became so pain-ridden I knew I couldn't put this mare through any further trials hoping for success. I left no stone unturned, but in the end I had a beautiful seven-year-old mare hardly able to walk to water on her own. Horses have a way of telling you when enough is enough.

Two young women who have gone through my Trainers Certification are like daughters to me. They saw the struggle in my heart and both came to help me through a difficult time. Through their caring and love they stayed with Lacee when the time came to end her pain. I didn't ask for their help, but they were brave and compassionate and I will be forever grateful to them, for being there for me, but most of all for being there for Lacee.

I have thought about Lacee a million times since that cold December day. I'm still touched by the compassion and love these young women showed for me, and my horse. Because of these two women, I felt a renewed sense of belief in mankind. Caring, compassion, and trust are vital as we make our way through this crazy thing we call life. Never underestimate the gift when you simply show you care to someone else.

CHAPTER 7

CHALLENGES

After meeting with some success, it's often difficult for a leader to uphold a high level of passion. One way to keep a fresh attitude, and not get in a rut, is to take on new challenges. My brain never stops working on new ideas for my business.

It's important not to get into a personal comfort zone. I work hard to be sure I take on new challenges, to test my limits, and often I discover the only limits are the ones I put on myself. Approaching a challenge with a fresh outlook and taking on new challenges isn't easy, but it can help you discover things about yourself you may have never known.

SKYDIVING:

In my twenties I wanted to try skydiving. Thinking about it and doing it are two very different things. Time went by and the moment passed. Thirty years later as I wrote a bucket list (yes, I have a bucket list!), skydiving appeared once again on my list to experience before I die. As fate would have it, my husband had skydiving on his list as well. We decided we'd check this challenge off both of our bucket lists in the summer.

At the local county fair/rodeo, in the distance we saw skydivers jumping out of planes from the local airport. We left the rodeo and headed for the airport. We found a skydiving club in the throes of their annual skydiving festival. We signed up to jump tandem the next day. Before I could digest what we were about to do, were promptly appointed a 10:00 a.m. jump the next morning.

I've worked with mental preparation and mental toughness over the years in my equine business. This wonderful opportunity tested my skills in this area. I slept great that night, but when I awoke the next morning I could feel a little twinge of anxiety emerging. On our drive into the airport, I knew I had to take control of my emotions or I'd never be able to jump out of an airplane.

It was an awesome experience, watching everyone *else* get ready for the jump. People of all ages would be jumping for the first time. Excitement was in the air, literally! As the plane climbed to our jumping altitude, I was excited but not scared. This challenge had eluded me for thirty years—and this was my moment. The door opened and out we went—. Amazing! The free fall was the best part! I took it all in. Every moment. Would I do it again, you bet!

Now I'm not saying go skydiving, but we all need to push ourselves and take on challenges that enable us to grow and learn.

In the past several years I've taken on such challenges as lecturing on leadership at colleges and large Equine events, showing in the NRHA, producing several audios, writing this book and, of course, skydiving. Each of these ventures taught me invaluable lessons about myself and about life.

THE CHALLENGE OF REINING:

When I decided to get involved with showing a reining horse, I knew very little about showing in these events. I'd shown in western pleasure and western trail, but never in an event that called for precision with speed. At first it was intimidating to be at these shows. There was so much to learn about the classes, rules, and judges and the learning curve of my horse and I working together as a team.

At the first several shows, I learned what a great group reining horse people truly are, helpful and supportive in every way. I learned about the scoring system and paid warm ups. (I'd never heard of paying for a five-minute time slot in the competition arena in my showing career of pleasure horses.)

I knew in order to be competitive, I needed a positive frame of mind and to look at every obstacle as an opportunity to grow. The year I began showing my reining horse, Ruff, was the most exciting and fulfilling time in my show career. The people I met were outstanding. I learned a ton about myself, and my new horse. I gained the confidence to move forward in many areas of my life, both in a business sense as well as personal.

Each new challenge brings personal growth. It's easy to get stuck in the familiar and predictable. When we begin to explore, open new doors, life can transform and give us gifts that otherwise we would never experience.

CHAPTER 8

COMMITMENT

Besides the commitment I have to my family I'm most committed to my profession as a horseman. If you look up the word *commitment* you'll find words like *promise, pledge,* and *obligation.* By working with horses and their owners it's instilled in me a commitment to always be honest, fair, and caring. Most horse owners want to do the right things for their horses. They want to learn how to be more effective in their communications skills and develop a good relationship with their horse. Oftentimes they are given poor advice from a well-meaning friend or possibly worked with a trainer who is more interested in the bottom line than being committed to teaching and educating both horse and rider. Anything worth having or doing in life requires time and commitment.

Where did I learn this lesson? How did I become a person to be trusted and committed in all areas of my life? From my mother. I've mentioned my mother before and I'm sure I will again. She was a strong role model and a huge influence in my life. I never doubted my mother or her commitment to me. I never doubted her support and because of that, I learned to never doubt myself as well. Her commitment to me made me a better person. When someone shows that kind of loyalty the result is courage to reach out and try new things. It's easy to be committed during good times, because when everything is going smoothly your commitment is never challenged. But loyalty and dedication during difficult times can be tough. My mother never wavered. When commitment doesn't waver that is the greatest part of the belief gift—all things are possible.

Mom would always tell me to follow my instincts and do what I love. Because of my mother's commitment to me, I'm able to be committed in my career and my personal life. Is there a down side to commitment? It's that I carry high standards not only for myself, but also for those around me. I fully expect my family, friends, and clients to show a high level of commitment to all that they vow.

I have a client who has been to every trainer, instructor, and clinician. She travels across the country riding in clinics with big name trainers and uses many different styles of training with her horses. When she came to me a few years ago she took some basic horsemanship lessons. She asked me a lot of questions based on the many different trainers she experienced. She was confused by the different approaches trainers shared with her. She did not know what to believe and what to dismiss.

There are many different approaches to anything in life and everyone has an opinion when it comes to horses. It's not necessarily a trainer, clinician, or friend is wrong. But at some point one must commit to studying under someone they trust so they gain the knowledge they seek. Then, we must give the method enough time to master and understand it. Once we have done that, then we can decide what we find valuable and what we might dismiss.

I took the John Lyons Certification Program in 1999. I was already training horses professionally, but I had watched John at several demonstrations and felt I could learn more. It was an intense program and took almost a year. I didn't agree with everything I learned, but as long as it wasn't harmful to me, or my horses, I stayed with it and graduated at the top of my class. I learned some wonderful tools and I grew as a horseman and as a person.

When people ask if I'm John Lyons Certified, I tend to cringe a little. Yes, I'm certified by John. But I've learned from some of the best trainers in the world. I still use bits and pieces of what John taught me, but I'd like to think I have developed enough of my own style. I no longer use *only* John's methodology. Was I committed to the John Lyons Certification? You bet! I'm also committed to being the best that I can be and staying true to who I am—Kathy Valentine, professional performance coach, horse trainer, clinician, and author.

When you commit, when you are dedicated and devoted, that's when the magic begins to unfold. It's during a time of commitment you begin to have a better understanding of who you are, and what you can accomplish. What a gift to give oneself!

CHAPTER 9

COMMUNICATION

Successful relationships begin and end with communication. The word *communication* means to convey a message. In order to communicate effectively with your friends, spouse, family or even your horse you must ask yourself three important questions.

- How do we talk to one another?
- How do we listen?
- What messages do I send to those around me?

Communication does not always come naturally; the good news is communication can be learned.

There are many different forms of communication. We convey messages through body language, eye contact, tone of voice, and facial expression, just to name a few. We live in a fast-paced world, where we e-mail, text, and often don't make physical contact with another person. The challenge in today's world is to not lose the art of communication because of the technology at our fingertips. I realize texting and e-mails are a form of communication. However, I'm referring to our most basic skills of communicating without technology.

Can you relate to the story of the man who is just getting home from work, he's met by his wife who simply gives him *that* look? You know the one. It says *you forgot today is our anniversary.* No words need to be spoken. The rigidity in her body language, torso turned away, and lips pursed. If she looks at him, her eyes are harsh. Everything in here screams, "Wow, you really messed up and I'm so not happy!" All without one word spoken.

Face-to-face contact with another person is vitally important in communication. Nothing can compare to that kind of interaction. I understand texting and e-mailing has its place, but I believe we must make a conscious effort to continue the skills of effective communication on a more personal level each day.

Horses are masters at reading body language. They can convey a message to another horse through a flick of an ear or a cock of a hip. Their moves are subtle yet another horse reads the message loud and clear. I've spent hours watching my horses interact. I love the way they speak through body language.

There is something in the way horses connect that allows us to get nearer to the natural world, something very instinctive, almost ancient, that takes us closer to the core of who we are. Humans need that primal connection, especially in today's fast-paced super high-tech world. There's a certain appeal of the "Western Lifestyle" because freedom, independence, and nature are associated to the idealistic way of life from yesteryear. And guess what, at the center of the western lifestyle is the horse.

Horses are wonderful for teaching people about leadership, communication, and healing one's soul. Horses bring us back to who we once were and ground us in an otherwise technological futuristic world.

Think about this, every piece of communication we send out starts with a thought. Have you ever watched someone who is deep in thought—and they smile? That smile is being communicated by the thought. Their entire body will lend itself to the thought. Everything from how they position their head and shoulders to the look in their eyes. All of it conveys a message. Our minds are powerful and we can choose how we will respond to something before we ever open our mouths.

Think about this: you're in the movie theater watching a scary movie. As the scene unfolds, adrenaline releases and your heart rate increases. You begin to twist in your seat. Soon as the scene intensifies, your body to tenses, you may even hold your breath. At the peak you may close your eyes—and scream.

But wait! Logically you're sitting in a movie theater safe and secure, yet your mind acted on received information. Your body reacted as if convinced the scene was real. That entire scenario is also true if you are reading a good book. The words cause you to feel a certain way. Imagine watching moviegoers watching different kinds of movies, scary to a sad drama to a documentary. By watching their body language, you would be able to tell what kind of a movie without ever seeing a scene yourself. That is communication through body language and the power of our mind.

Horse people talk about being able to "read a horse". Being able to read a horse means intuitively understanding what the horse is thinking before he physically does something. The challenge is discerning the differences between a horse pinning his ears in anger versus the horse in pain. Or the horse that turns his rump toward you—is he going to kick or does he want you to scratch him?

It sounds pretty simple, but there's an art to reading horses. The art is learning to understand, and feel, the unspoken language of communication. A horse cannot say, "my back hurts" or "I'm so angry at you for blah-blah-blah." In order for us to have a relationship with the horse, we must get better at listening to the subtleties of their body language.

It's really no different with people. If we tune in and practice becoming aware, our ability to communicate will grow immensely. As we learn to read others through different types of communication skills, we must also become aware of the messages we send out to others.

Good communication skills take practice. We have opportunities everywhere to learn and grow every day in a wide variety of situations. Tomorrow will you take time to watch and listen and learn from those around you? It can happen at the store, the bank, the gas station, the work place, school and especially at home with those you love.

Communication is simply another word for connecting. I hope I connected with you as you read this chapter. I hope my skills of communication reach out and touch you. You are an incredible human being. Trust in your journey!

CHAPTER 10

CONSCIENCE

The definition of *conscience*: the sense of right and wrong that governs a person's thoughts and actions, urging him or her to do right rather than wrong. As I read this definition, I understood that a person's compass of right and wrong will be determined by what their beliefs are and how they see the world.

We would like to think there are certain areas everyone agrees are right and wrong. That these areas are black and white; however when it seems crystal clear, often it's a matter of interpretation by the individual.

I've been training horses for many years. When asked about my training program, I give a general overview. For instance, I work a horse in training five days a week. I generally work a horse at least one hour a day. That changes based on the horse's needs. I feed a quality grass hay and vitamin supplements. Horses are fed four times a day. All paddocks are cleaned seven days a week. No one but me handles a horse in training. I have an open barn policy—if your horse is in training, you can visit anytime without an appointment.

When someone brings a horse to me I understand the huge responsibility to take good care of my client's horse and have integrity in everything I do with him. My word is valuable. If I said I'm going to do something, I absolutely will do it. If I'm running late, my conscience always speaks to me. I need to be truthful and give 110%. My conscience won't allow me to ignore the promise. My conscience guides me to always do the right thing even when no one is watching. It's a part of who I am.

Some potential clients haven't had the same level of conscientiousness. A prospective new client might tell me a horse has had no issues such as biting, kicking, or bucking but when I do my evaluation on the horse it's clear these problems do exist.

When confronted on the issue, an owner might lie by omission. I've been amazed at how many people have been less than honest about a very dangerous horse and still sleep knowing they did not tell me about the danger.

I recently did demonstrations at a local horse exposition in Belgrade, Montana. It was a weekend event and I had several horses to work with. One mare, the people claimed to have purchased from a sale, but no one had any knowledge of this mare's history. They didn't know her level of training or whether she was broke to ride. My job was to do an evaluation on this mare.

I asked a lot of questions before I began handling this horse. Supposedly someone worked with this horse a week earlier and stated the horse did great, fine both on the ground and under saddle. I then discovered they were trying to sell this mare to a woman at this event. A red flag went up because of the unwillingness on the part of the current owner to share information with me about this horse. It reminded me of a sticky horse. Sticky is a term horseman use to describe a horse that doesn't give 100% but gets stuck, and gives up on occasion, causing the rider to have to work harder to convince the horse to keep trying.

I began my demonstration by doing a series of exercises on the ground to learn about the mare's willingness to work with someone. She was fairly quiet but had a feeling of disconnect with her handler. After twenty minutes of groundwork, I asked for a bridle. The mare took the bit easily, but when I went to apply a little pressure to the rein she reared up and back violently. I let her settle down and asked again, up and back she went, her breathing was rapid and she was tense.

I explained to the audience that this mare would have the same response under saddle. My guess was that she had a severe rearing issue and most likely would flip over with her rider. This seemed an ingrained behavior in this horse's mind.

I opted not to saddle and mount this horse for obvious reasons. I continued to work her on the ground and finished my demonstration. I learned later the mare had a history of rearing and flipping over. The current owners were well aware but hadn't shared this information. How could anyone allow another human being to risk injury or even death and knowingly not share that information? Did they not have a conscience? How does one go to sleep at night knowing they've been less than honest, and because of their lack of honesty, my life could have been changed in a heartbeat? One could argue I was the trainer and it was my job to deal with this mare. However I had asked many questions before my session with her. The answers I received were clearly untruthful and misleading.

I wish I could say that was a rare and isolated case, but the truth is I have seen it often in my career. What causes one to have such high standards and another seems to have no conscience at all? I'm a firm believer that life constantly offers us opportunities to learn, grow, and change for the better. Maybe you'll read this and think, *gosh I need to do better and think more about my actions and how they affect others around me.* Or maybe you understand the principles of right and wrong, but have the opportunity to mentor someone that may not. Whichever path you are on, I hope you'll take some time to think about that inner voice that says do the right thing, the good thing, the honest thing. Listen carefully to that voice and let it be heard.

CHAPTER 11

CONSISTENCY

Consistency is the ability to maintain a particular standard or repeat a particular task with minimal variation.

I've always admired horsemen who are consistent with their horses. I refer to the consistency of how they cue their horses for different maneuvers to having a thought-out, structured riding program offered on a regular basis. Being consistent and fair is what allows a horse to relax and want to give 110% on every ride. It's no different for people. People who are consistent in their behavior and fair in their actions help us relax because we can trust them.

In my early teens my mother remarried and moved us to Deep River, Connecticut. For a young girl who'd grown up in the same small town, going to the same school, with the same friends, my world turned upside down. My mom recognized this would be a difficult change for me. She made sure I could keep my horses and she worked hard at being supportive. That wasn't an easy task for someone who worked third shift at a hospital with a two-hour commute. We no longer had enough property for the horses, so they had to be boarded at a small private barn. At the time I didn't understand the sacrifices my mother had to make so that we could board them. I wasn't an easy child. I was strong-willed and after the move I began to regress and act out.

I just didn't fit in. That was how I felt. I simply did not connect with my new school or anyone in my new neighborhood. I knew exactly where I did fit in—with my horses. Every day I'd wait for the bus to pick me up. I rode all the way to the school and then walked off into the woods. I'd discovered a way to hike through the forest and get to the barn where my horses boarded. Because it was a small private facility, no one was there during school hours. I'd have the entire day to myself to hang out with my three horses and then get back to my bus stop and walk home. Guess I hadn't thought about the school contacting my mother when I wasn't there day after day.

One evening my mom sat me down, "How's school going?"

"Fine."

She looked me in the eyes. "The principal called from the school and told me you have not been to any classes in a week."

I knew I had to fess up. I cried. I was angry and sad.

Mom listened. She always took time to listen, always stayed calm and composed. That day was no different. She was a safe place for me. Safe because she was consistent in her actions, consistent to love and listen and care about me, consistent in always being fair.

It wasn't an easy adjustment for me. Seven more times I skipped school and went to the barn. As a matter of fact, I missed a total of fifty-seven days of school that year. Mom helped me the best way she knew how. She understood my connection with my horses. She knew I felt safe and accepted by them and she also knew it was only a matter of time before I'd come around and figure out how to connect with my new life.

Now I realize how important it is to build relationships, to know enough about that individual or that horse so we can nurture them and offer good advice. What if my mother had taken a different path? What if she'd said, "Fine Kathryn, I'm not going to allow you to see your horses until you straighten out"

The outcome would have been so different. But that year I became an honor student, made a lot of friends, and graduated with honors from Valley Regional High School in Deep River,

Connecticut. My mother taught me about consistency, reliability, and stability. She taught me about loyalty and commitment and being someone others can count on. My mom taught me an invaluable lesson that year, one I carry on with my spouse, my friends, my business, and my horses.

CHAPTER 12

COURAGE

*"Courage is the first of human qualities because it's the
quality which guarantees the others."*—Aristotle

You can possess many good qualities but if you don't have the
courage to move forward you may never see those qualities
develop. It takes courage to put yourself out there for the world
to see, it takes courage to stand up for something you believe in,
it takes courage to believe in yourself. Courage is daring to turn
your dream into a reality.

Many people allow fear to get in the way of pursuing a dream
or goal. How sad fearfulness will limit what some people achieve
in life: therefore, affecting ones happiness and self-worth.

I travel and conduct workshops and clinics for horsemanship
and leadership. The one common denominator I see repeatedly is
people who want to participate in the clinic but do not have the
courage to face their fears. Fear of looking silly, or not being able
to perform a task, fear of failure, fear of others judgment. The list
goes on and on.

It takes courage to overcome the emotional and mental
obstacles we create. The payoff is monumental. Each new lesson
we learn on facing our fears, and the courage to pursue a goal, we

build a history of confidence that we can achieve and when we don't succeed, we are still okay.

When I'm working with students and know they'll have to move out of their comfort zone, I tell them the situation at hand is an opportunity to learn and experience something new. Maybe it's an opportunity to teach their horse something he needs to experience. When faced with something they fear, if I can show a student how much it will help their horses learn to trust and become more courageous, nine out of ten times people will to face their own fears out of loyalty to their horses. The byproduct of this experience is the handler/rider builds confidence, not only with their horses, in all areas.

I was recently asked to be a featured speaker at The Equine Affaire in Pomona, California. I do a fair amount of public speaking but had never lectured at an Equine Affaire. I suppose I'd created this image of the event being bigger and more powerful than myself. I had two lectures to give, one was called, *Actions Speak Louder Than Words: the subtleties of body language*, and the second, *Managing Pre-Show Jitters*.

Although it was an honor for me to be asked to do these lectures, I also faced the fear of failure. All the "what-ifs" raced into my mind. What if the crowd didn't like me? What if I forgot what to say in the middle of my talk? What if no one came to hear me? What if . . . what if . . . what if . . .

I could have allowed the fear and apprehension to take over and decline the offer to speak. Or I could find the inner strength to move forward, do the best job I could, and remember this was an opportunity to grow and learn as a person and as a speaker.

I went to the event and I faced my fears. It wasn't a perfect performance. My anxiety was high but I found the courage to try something new. The show management gave me an out of the way location at a 6:00 p.m. time slot, which took place at the same time as the Trail Challenge in the main arena. The Trail Challenge was the biggest event that weekend. I was feeling a bit nervous as I waited for the bleachers to fill.

When I began my first lecture I had ten people attending. For a moment I wanted to cancel; that would be the easy way out. I wouldn't have to face such embarrassment and emotional distress. As quickly as those thoughts came to mind, I pushed them away and replaced them with the thoughts of opportunity. This was a chance to share with others my beliefs and ideas about competing. I even managed to find some humor in the situation. Though I only had ten people, all ten were extremely interested in what I had to share. They stayed well after my lecture to continue asking questions and telling me how much they enjoyed my talk. I took away some valuable lessons that weekend.

As a teacher, I must push myself to experience the same doubts and fears my students do. This humbles and reminds me what it feels like to experience those emotions. It keeps my teaching real and allows my students to know I don't simply talk-the-talk, I walk-the-walk. Having someone who has shared similar trials allows us to connect in a deeper fashion. It also helps me to better understand and assist my students in overcoming their worries. Getting out of my comfort zone allows me to give students the tools they need to have courage and strength to pursue and move forward in their riding and life.

CHAPTER 13

CRISIS

As a professional horse trainer I'm often asked by my clients, "What do I do when I'm riding in a new area with my horse and he begins to act out of control. It feels unsafe and I feel like we are in the middle of a crisis?"

My response is always the same: "What are you doing riding in a new or unfamiliar area if you do not feel you have the tools in place to handle any situation?"

A crisis is not handled at the moment it occurs. A crisis is prepared for by the history you've built with your horse and in yourself. Trust and good communication must be in place before the crisis occurs. Prepare for the crisis well ahead of time by building a strong relationship based on mutual respect, trust, and confidence. For me every ride, every interaction with my horse builds preparation in the horse and me for everything and anything. I don't need to desensitize my horse to everything. I find no need to show him fifty different things and force him to "get used to it." I cannot control the million different scenarios that might scare or bother my horse. What I can control is my communication with him. When I pick up a rein and ask him to stop, back, drop his head, soften, etc., he'll do so without question because he understands what I want. My horse can trust I've always been fair to him. Once those tools are in place, only then do I begin to ride in areas that could hold an unforeseen crisis. At that point I feel confident my horse and I are a team and we can safely enjoy riding in any environment with the knowledge we can trust each other at a moment's notice. Remember trust goes both ways.

A crisis can cause people to go into a defensive mode and they forget their horse is a part of the equation. If we have not trained ourselves to handle adversity then how can we expect our horses to stay calm and think through the crisis situation?

When things are calm and relaxed it's easy to stay in control and be thoughtful and easy going. When things get dangerous, frightening, and complex our authentic self emerges. It's during those moments we need to have the skills in place to handle a crisis. We must be prepared mentally, emotionally, and physically to handle a difficult situation.

MENTAL TOUGHNESS IN ACTION

Last fall I took a young horse in to start under saddle and had put several rides on him in my arena. He was a quiet easy-going colt and I felt fine about riding him that day. I went out to the arena and spent about ten minutes on the ground working this colt with the saddle and bridle on. As I went to step up into the saddle he moved off. He wasn't scared or bothered, he simply moved. I picked up the rein to stop him (which he did nicely). However, I needed to take a hop-step to get closer. As I did, I realized my foot was stuck in the stirrup. When I took the hop, it spooked him. I remember feeling him pull me off my feet. I remember thinking he could kick me in the face. He took off around the arena. It was as if everything was in slow motion. Because of training, I became very calm and relaxed. I told myself to relax my foot so it could come out of the boot. Within a few strides I was free from the stirrup and lying unharmed on the ground.

In thirty years of teaching and training horses I'd never had that happen before. I know because I have the mental, emotional, and physical skills in place, and practiced in a variety of situations, that training saved me from what could have been a horrific accident. In a crisis moment my skills, trust in myself, and ability to stay calm and focused saved my life. I wasn't angry at the colt because the accident wasn't his fault. There was no one to blame. It was simply a crisis moment and I'm thankful I had the skills to see it through.

Here is the good news. The skills I'm talking about are skills everyone can and should learn. As I reflect on many things in my life, both in and out of the horse world, I'm reminded that no one skill we learn, no one lesson is ever just about that isolated moment. It's so much bigger. Those are the building blocks that teach us how to become stronger emotionally, mentally, and physically for the journey ahead.

There are opportunities everyday that help guide us and prepare us for those difficult times. I tell my students they need to become aware of those opportunities and utilize them. Learn from them. Be grateful for them. Becoming strong in communication, emotional control, and learning skills to trust yourself and others prepares each of us for handling a crisis with our horses, at home, with our family members, and even at our place of business.

CHAPTER 14

ENTHUSIASM

Enthusiasm is having a great interest or passion. Enthusiastic people generate an excitement and may feel invincible. Emotion is a driving force. A positive emotion like enthusiasm causes those around to capture that energy as well.

I began teaching my Equine Apprenticeship Program twelve years ago in Mount Vernon, Washington. My first year implementing this program, I knew I'd need to adjust as I tested ideas. A young student taking lessons decided she would like to take the program with her Arab colt, Sequoia. Katie was eighteen and had a passion to learn about training horses. She was a beautiful young woman; smart, talented and enthusiastic. The program met once a week for several hours of hands on training. The student then has one week to master those lessons before the next series of training.

Each week Katie and Sequoia would meet with me at my arena. We'd start the session with basic warm up exercises and then a demonstration from Katie of what the two had accomplished. The first several weeks, when she would show me what they had learned, I thought this course was too easy—she nailed everything I'd shown her. I decided to challenge her even more.

Over the next several weeks Katie shone. She always had a smile and enthusiasm. Even on weeks that she struggled to figure out a new maneuver, Katie's attitude and passion shone through. She was determined to do her best and to help her horse excel in his training.

Katie did not know the gift she gave to me. Katie made teaching fun and challenging. I looked forward to meeting with her every week eager to share all I could. Her enthusiasm made me enthusiastic. I couldn't help but get caught up in her positive energy and become as passionate as Katie. She also gave me the desire to pursue this new program—she gave me hope this program could and would be a success.

The Practical Apprenticeship Program has been in place now for twelve consecutive years. I'm proud of how it's developed and continues to make a difference to the graduates. Katie continues to be a dear friend. She's now married with three children. Her passion and enthusiasm for horses and teaching others is still alive and well. I'm so very proud of this young woman on every level.

I kept an e-mail I received from Katie's dad after Katie attended my program:

"Kathy,

"I want to thank you for coming out and doing the clinic. It was great. I enjoyed it immensely. I learned so much over the weekend. It was also great watching and feeling Willow responding to the cues. It finally clicked in my head what I was doing wrong and what I needed to do to correct it. She was very soft and wasn't as confused as to what I was asking. It also made it enjoyable to ride her. I've been working Willow and am now able to get a canter very easily now. The things I've learned from you have made me a better rider. It's appreciated.

The main thing I want to thank you for, even though thank you seems inadequate, is the difference your mentoring Katie has made for her. It's really built her confidence in all aspects of her life. She struggled in school because of her dyslexia, and didn't get much support from her teachers.

> *In fact one teacher told us that she didn't see much of a future for Katie. We pulled her out and home schooled from then until high school. Most of what she learned at home centered on horses. The opportunity to participate in your first apprenticeship program helped her blossom as a young woman. As her father, I can't even begin to describe the joy I get from watching her work with her horse and others who struggle getting their horses to respond in a positive way. I know God puts people in our lives to help us grow and mature. You have been one such person in the life of my daughter. For that I'm forever grateful!*
>
> *Sincerely, Ken"*

I had no idea that Katie had been labeled with a learning disability. This young woman is bright, creative, and passionate. It's a reminder that in those moments of passion and enthusiasm, our gifts and talents reveal who we truly are.

CHAPTER 15

FAILURE

Failure is a harsh word. When emotion connects to the word *failure*, we often feel sad and defeated. Failure implies an ending rather than a beginning. I found it very difficult to include a chapter with the title *Failure* on it. I realized I've disciplined myself to think in the positive. The mere suggestion of the word failure is offensive to my senses. I encourage you to practice thinking in the positive. Allowing the emotion attached to the word to be negative, and the impact is devastating. However, change that emotion to a temporary disappointment and add the knowledge you've learned from it, then failure takes on an entirely different value.

I wasn't always a positive thinker. As a matter of fact, in my twenties I was a somewhat negative and pessimistic person. I'm not suggesting I was never happy or positive. When things were going well, I was as happy and upbeat as anyone could be. On the other hand, when challenged outside my comfort zone, I could be quite self-destructive. Rather than putting myself out there and trying something new, I'd avoid the challenge, or better yet, come up with excuses why I couldn't participate. When things are going well it's always easier to be upbeat and positive than when we are faced with adversity.

My and mother and grandmother told me challenges, and even failing, would bring me wisdom and growth. They'd say, "It's an opportunity to learn and grow."

At that time in my life, I just didn't get it. The words made sense but applying the strategy to my life was much more difficult. I was very critical about myself and the feeling associated with failure was unbearable. So unbearable it seemed easier to protect myself and not try something new so I would not be faced with the possibility of failing.

I've always had a passion for horses. Riding and showing, but I was intrigued with the horse itself. I loved studying the horse and his interaction with other horses as well as with humans. I wanted to better understand the subtleties of their communication and the magical sense I felt in their presence.

I began showing horses at an early age. From lead line class to competing in youth classes, I never did excel in showing as a child or young adult. I placed but rarely won first or high point. I'd blame my horse—he was spooky that day or off somehow. If he would just pay attention to me, he's always so great at home . . . It's the wind, or the footing, or the judge doesn't like us. The list went on and on. Funny, back then I convinced myself those statements were true. I, in no way looked at myself, or the part I might play. (Another reason I so admire the horse his patience and humbleness not to take things personally, but allow his rider time to grow and learn.)

And I did learn. I learned to lighten up and have fun. I learned it was okay to make a mistake as long as I learned a lesson from it. I also learned to look at the part I play in my horse's life, and in the lives of those around me. What a gift when I began to see myself in a different light! I began to take responsibility for my actions and grow as a person. Maybe Mom and Grandma were right after all; failing is simply a bump in the road preparing us for whatever lies ahead, an opportunity to grow and learn.

As time went on I considered myself a good horseman, but I also knew my limits. When I received a phone call from my friend Dennis, who asked me to help his daughter load a horse in their trailer, I hesitated. I was in my early twenties and although good at many aspects of training, I had yet to work with difficult or dangerous horses. Certainly not horses that needed to learn how to load quietly into a horse trailer. The mere thought of this challenge was an adrenaline rush. I was excited, scared, and driven. Would I succeed or fail? What was the big deal? It was just a trailer loading.

When I arrived, I noticed there were a lot of cars parked at the equine facility. I was quite sure there was no show that day. I assumed it was just a nice day and people were out enjoying their horses.

Dennis met me. "I hope you don't mind some of the boarders wanted to watch. We've been trying to load this horse for months and no one has been successful."

Oh my, note to self, never assume anything. "Sure Dennis, no problem . . ." The pressure was on. We walked over to the horse trailer. Twenty-five to thirty people gathered around with their lawn chairs to watch me load this little mare. I could hear them laughing and taking bets.

Dennis' daughter, Morgan, walked her mare out from the barn to the trailer. She told me she wanted to show her horse but the trailer loading issues stood in her way. This poor child looked so defeated. She told me of many attempts to teach her horse to load, from butt ropes (this is when two people hold ends of a rope and try to force a horse into the horse trailer while a third person pulls on a lead rope in front of the horse) to parking the trailer in the field with the mare's hay inside hoping she'd get hungry and go into the trailer. Then there was the story of pitchforks, yes pitchforks and whips. Yet no one could load this little mare.

I could see the fear in both the eyes of the child and the horse as they wondered what my tactic would be. There was almost a pleading from Morgan to, please, not hurt her horse. I gave Morgan a hug and told her I would be patient, firm, and fair. As I took the lead rope and lead the little mare toward the trailer, I doubted myself terribly and hoped it did not show.

In less than one hour Morgan's little mare stood quietly in the trailer. In two hours I'd taught Morgan how to cue her horse to load every time. By now most of the folks had left. I guess they were hoping for more of a rodeo and maybe a bit put out that their bets were ill placed. A few stopped by and said, "Good job." Most importantly, that day I learned about myself. I learned to trust myself more and to remember that this experience was worth its weight in gold. Sure, it was a great outcome. But to get to it I had to rise to the occasion and take the chance. I also learned that I never wanted to be like folks who thrived off of someone else's possible failure. I wanted to be a person who encourages others and wants them to succeed.

That trailer loading was a turning point in my career. I wanted to make a positive difference in the lives of horses and their owners. I went on to become certified by John Lyons and have worked with many prestigious show trainers as I continued to learn and grow as a horseman. Interestingly enough I've gained respect and often asked at horse events to demonstrate my trailer loading technique. It's become my favorite demonstration.

None of us ever know what opportunities lay ahead and sometimes we must challenge ourselves to find out. This reminds me of a saying I once heard: "Sometimes you have to take the leap and build your wings on the way down." I hope you'll learn to take that leap even if it turns out to be a stumble. You'll land and learn wonderful lessons from the experience. Lessons that help build strength for your dreams.

Morgan and her dad moved away not long after that trailer event. We lost contact for many years. Several years ago Morgan e-mailed. She thanked me for what I'd done for her and that little mare fifteen years earlier. She told how she used that lesson on other horses and she wondered if I remembered her.

Yes, Morgan I remember.

CHAPTER 16

FAMILY

I grew up in Connecticut as the youngest of four children. My mother was a nurse's aid at Lawrence Memorial Hospital in New London, Connecticut, and my dad was a commercial painter and steel worker. I wish I could tell you that I had a warm and loving family and that we were close and happy. My mother was a great mom. She was the hardest worker I have ever known and loved her children deeply. My dad, on the other hand, was a heavy drinker and physically and emotionally abusive to my mother and my brother Tom. My other two siblings were grown, so as best I can recall they were not a part of his abusive ways. My dad was very loving and kind to me, I was often referred to as Daddy's Girl. I'm not sure why I was the chosen one for his times of kindness.

My father was harsh in his words and actions. On several occasions he held my mother down and threatened her life. I'd run into their bedroom and beg my dad to leave her alone. If that were not enough, he'd tell Mom how unattractive she was or tell her to lose weight. I can also recall a terrifying event were Dad took a hatchet and put hundreds of holes in my bedroom wall in a fit of anger. He even cut a pin in half I'd given to my mother as a Christmas gift.

My childhood was filled with fear and anxiety. We never knew what might set my father off. I cried myself to sleep many nights feeling scared and powerless. My saving grace—our horses. One of my favorite first memories was Dad putting me up in front, on the saddle with him, on his big sorrel horse, Red. I was probably two at the time. We galloped through the woods to visit one of his friends. On the way he stopped and broke off a piece of birch from a tree for me to chew. It tasted like root beer!

My dad showed horses in an event called Gymkana. A variety of timed events where rider and horse followed a specific pattern around barrels or poles. He was very good at these events. It wasn't long before he bought my first pony. So began my infatuation with horses. He was a Shetland pony and I named him Little Bit. I remember my dad took the back seat out of our station wagon and loaded the pony so I could go to a show. Oftentimes the judge would give me a trophy just because Little Bit and I were so cute together.

I might have had a challenging father but I was also blessed with a wonderful Mom and siblings. My sister Linda is fourteen years older than myself. She reminds me of my Mother, Aunt Margaret and Grandmother all wrapped up into one. She is beautiful on the inside and out. She is devoted to family and has a strong spiritual belief. She is a passionate, confident and vibrant woman. When I was a small child I would sometimes become jealous of her because everyone in my family referred to Linda as the good daughter, she could do no wrong. She never created a scene and was always there when someone needed something. (I had a bit more renegade approach to life at times!) That jealousy turned into admiration as I grew up and became a young adult. She was my role model, teaching me about forgiveness and teaching me to see the beauty in every human being. Linda would tell you that she remembers my Dad in a very different way. He was a good man who loved his children. Her memories are much happier than mine and I love to hear the stories she tells of him because I realize that what may have been my reality is not the whole story.

My brother Hyde, "Bub" is ten years older than I. He reminds me of my Uncle Arthur who is gentle, kind and soft spoken. Bub is the story teller of the family. One never knows what wild story Bub will come up with and he loves to get a rise from whomever he is telling it to. Bub is also an equine enthusiast a gift both Mom and Dad blessed us with. Bub is also a lot like my Dad when it comes to authority. He likes to paint outside the lines and then debate why it should be any different. Now that I think of it all of us kids are like that! It just made me smile because I do not always think of the good traits my Dad gave to each one of us. I can tell you that as I wrote this book and took the time to reflect and talk to my siblings I have a new sense of love and compassion for my Dad.

Last but not least is my brother Tom. He is eight years older than I am. He is my Dad inside and out. He walks like him, talks like him and looks like him. Tom is a loving and kind man. He is always willing to challenge those who play by the rules and has a strong opinion about the world we live in. He adores his children and granddaughter and has a wonderful love for his family. He shares a passion for animals and was also a horseman. Tom and I were always close. We were the last two children living at home when my Mom and Dad divorced. Those where some hard times but Tom always had his baby sisters back. Now some forty years later he still has my back.

The point I am trying to make here is that we all have our opinion of what family means. We will all use different words to describe it. My lesson in this is to remember that each of us brings our own story to the table. My perception is just that, it's mine not necessarily my families. Each of my siblings will have their own memories and opinion of what our family was like. I was not always at a place in my life where I could hear what they each had to say especially about my Dad but I have grown to understand and to accept that life is a journey and I must celebrate and embrace the lessons I am learning each day. To all of my siblings I love you!

Looking back the memories with my horses supersede many of the struggles of a difficult parent. Thank God my mother was emotionally strong, positive, and a gentle spirit. She divorced my dad when I was nine. I watched her struggles and triumphs as she made her way on her own, raising her children. The lessons she taught have carried me through life and continue to bless me even now at fifty. She taught me to be kind to others, have patience, and a loving heart. My mother gave me the gift of being authentic. Through authenticity comes creativity and confidence.

It was a hardship for her to keep horses a part of my life at a time when she was struggling to keep food on the table. I wonder how she supported my horses as well. But she always made sure I had my horse and even managed to keep that little Shetland pony until he died twenty-five years later. My mother recognized the importance of having horses in my life. She knew they would carry a young girl through the hard times and teach her lessons like no human.

We all have choices we make in our lives. We can choose to be happy and successful or we can choose to be a victim. I could have sung the *poor me* song. Mine wasn't a story of the happy all-American family. I could have chosen to be angry and depressed and blame others for my misfortunes. Or I could choose not to allow my past to define me. All the hardships I endured are building blocks to become an independent, strong, and confident woman. I have no bitterness about my past.

Thirty years after my parents divorced, my father was lying on his deathbed with my siblings by his side. My mother walked into that room and stood over dad. She took his hand and leaned over him. With all her gentleness and kindness, she told him she forgave him. He squeezed her hand and within moments he went to be with the Lord. You see, I choose to be a part of that beautiful woman; that was my mother, and I'm proud to be her daughter. I also choose to be a part of the goodness that was inside the man I know as my father.

As I go through my life I choose to remember the good times, the peaceful times. If you come from a loving and wonderful family, celebrate that blessing. Hold them close in your heart. If you come from a broken or abusive home, choose to be strong and whole. Choose the wonderful life that can, and should, be yours.

CHAPTER 17

FRIENDSHIP

A friend is a wonderful gift and one of the best gifts you can be. We'll meet many people throughout our lives. Some will be there for a season some for much longer. Some friends will be there forever.

In Connecticut, working as a professional horse trainer, I received a phone call from a woman who needed help with a recently purchased horse. We met and talked about my training philosophies and how I might help her. Soon after that meeting, Shirley started taking lessons with her Morgan gelding, Younger. After several months of lessons, Shirley and I developed a friendship.

One beautiful summer day, I asked Shirley if she'd like to come along on a trail ride. On our way, I needed to make one more stop to drop off my new puppy at my mom's house. I introduced Mom and Shirley. They visited for a few minutes and then we were back on the road.

As we drove to the trail Shirley said, "Where does your mom work?"

"Lawrence Memorial Hospital."

"What floor?"

"E-3," I said.

She smiled. "Is her best friend Barbara Tirrell?"

"YES, how do you know her?"

"She's my mom. She's been telling me for years about Mary, and how her daughter is into horses."

Mary, my mom, had also mentioned she'd like me to meet Barbara's daughter because *she* was into horses. This story is one of our favorite stories to tell. Our moms were best friends. They traveled together and were very close. Shirley and I have been blessed with the same kind of friendship. We've been there for each other, in good times and bad, and continue to talk weekly on the phone. We meet each year for a vacation/get together.

Shirley lost her Mom to cancer some years ago. In 2005 I lost my Mom as well to that hideous disease. Shirley was there for me each step of the way. I would've been lost without her.

When I decided to attend the John Lyons certification in Parachute, Colorado, it was Shirley who rode shotgun. Shirley helped me turn that dream into a reality.

In 2007 Shirley and I rode the Outlaw Trail Ride in Wyoming. It's weeklong 100-mile ride that hosts 100 people. We have many wonderful stories about that ride. I can't think of a single person I'd have wanted more next to me, sleeping in a one-man tent for a week!

Building history with someone is vital. Through that history comes a deep bond and trust. That's also true of our horses. Many times I hear people say, "I love my horse. I brush him and feed him but he doesn't seem to trust me."

My response to this is build good history; history isn't sitting on the couch every night watching TV with someone. History is getting out and experiencing life together. It's learning about one another in all of life's circumstances, the good the bad and the ugly.

Look at the history Shirley and I have developed. We have had the best of times together and been there for the worst of times. I feel the same with my horses. I own a little reining horse that was a full-time show horse until this year. I decided to give him a much-needed break and take him trail riding for the entire summer. Our history until now was in the show pen. We trust one another completely in that environment. Being out on the trail has been an eye opening experience for both of us. Up until this point my show horse was sure the world was flat and had perfect footing! Trust on both our parts is limited when we're faced with the obstacles on a trail ride. A fascinating and fun experience as Ruff and I build trust and history on the mountain trails.

We came upon a downed tree. It was up to Ruffs chest so I got off and encouraged my reining horse to jump the tree. The look on his face was priceless. He had a look of disbelief, but he did it. Then about an hour later he got a rock stuck in his shoe and stood three-legged with a similar look of disbelief on his face. I pulled the rock out and we were on our way. We crossed bridges and raging water, climbed steep and narrow trails, with each obstacle we worked together as a team. I'm always patient with Ruff as he figures out what to do. I have learned how willing and honest he is as our trust grows in each other. It's an amazing journey to build relationships both equine and human.

I have several very dear friends. I take our friendships seriously; they are my family, my heart, and soul. I hope I have been as good a friend to Shirley as she has been to me. Shirley, if you are reading this book, thanks for being you. Love you.

CHAPTER 18

GRATITUDE

Gratitude means to be grateful, to give thanks. Good times make it easy to be upbeat and thankful for what we have. When things are going really great we often forget just how fortunate we are. As humans it's so easy to take things for granted.

I'm no different than anyone. I've run through the cycles of grateful, then taking things for granted, followed by the occasional *why me?* moments. My mother was diagnosed with colon cancer in 2002. The doctors gave her one to three years. She made a move from Connecticut to Montana to be close to me.

I was thrilled to have my mom living so close. For three years we enjoyed each other's company. She watched as my business grew and cheered me on when I built my indoor arena. She told everyone, "My daughter will be famous someday." You know how moms can be! We had a regular routine of meeting and driving to Missoula once a week for shopping and lunch. On Wednesday evenings during the winter we played cards. As soon as spring was in the air, my mother would say, "No more cards. My garden needs attention."

In December of 2004 my mother took a turn for the worse. The cancer was spreading and she needed chemo yet again. The doctors were less than positive. She fought a hard fight, my mom did. She finally quit chemo in May of 2005. She realized she would not survive the summer.

These were hard times. My sister, brother, step-dad, and I joined forces to take care of her. Somehow, even when you know time is limited, and the moment will arrive when your loved one will leave, you are just never prepared.

July 29th, 2005, we all stood at my mother's bedside. I was held her hand when she took her final breath. I whispered, "Oh Mom—"

Eight months of struggling were over for her. But for those left behind the struggles just began.

When someone is sick, we manage to fill the hole with being a caretaker. Though the lifestyle has changed we manage to make a new normal. But now there would be no caretaking, no round the clock vigils. What now?

I went home numb. It wasn't at all real. By late evening I was sobbing uncontrollably. I didn't think I'd ever get over this horrible pain. Through it all my wonderful Australian Shepherd, Seattle, stayed close by me. He was quiet but made sure he physically touched me. I sobbed most of the night. I thought I might just die—die of a broken heart. In the early morning I knew I had to get control, find a way to get some peace, and relief from my grief.

My mother's rosary beads hung on the bedpost. I picked them up and recited the rosary. I went through twice. On my third attempt, I changed my prayers. I said one thing I was grateful for with each bead—no matter how big or small. I'm grateful for my dog, Seattle, lying here beside me. I'm thankful my family stayed by my mom's side. I'm grateful for the sunrise, the cool morning air, the clouds, the wind, the grass and trees. I'm grateful I live in Montana. I'm grateful, I had the best Mom ever. I'm grateful she left behind a legacy of honesty, courage, trust, confidence, gentleness, beauty and grace. The list went on and on. No longer sobbing, I was focused on the good still in my life.

I changed that day. I realized that it's during the most difficult times, the most complex, and truly cruel and unforgiving times we must find peace in gratitude. Oh, I still miss my mom. Almost daily I think of her, but I'm reminded when I say my gratitude beads (my rosary) of all my blessings. I've learned to find peace again in my heart. I also learned the importance of giving thanks every single day—not just during the joyful and wonderful times, but during the hard times too. I made a daily ritual to take my rosary and give thanks, one bead at a time, every day.

CHAPTER 19

GUIDANCE

Throughout life we assume different roles. This holds true for the roles of student versus teacher. Sometimes we're the one guiding and sometimes we're the one being guided. We must honor each role in order to gain the most insight.

"Become a student of life." Everyday holds opportunities to learn. There's never a situation in which we cannot learn something. They key is how we choose to handle the moment. We need to learn to stay open, and non-defensive, when things are not exactly the way we want them to be. Our egos, and sometimes the feeling of a lack of control, can get in our way.

I was asked to do some lectures on leadership for the Forest Service in Montana. An interesting forum a brilliant woman, Bernadette Bannister, who works for the University of Montana, created. She had a vision of setting up leadership classes by introducing three people who were specialists in their field. There was a professional dog trainer, professional martial arts instructor, and myself, a specialist on equines and human relationships.

Her idea put three experts on body language and leadership in place. Each created a workshop to teach the students skills they could use in the workplace, in everyday situations, as well as in their personal lives. I've been a part of this unique program for four years and I have found it to be an exceptional and informative opportunity.

Bernadette is the facilitator and does a wonderful job linking the three experts together with some of her own real life situations. It's creative, inspiring and motivating. What a great gift Bernadette has given to the Forest service, their leadership workshop, and all three speakers. We all share and learn from such a unique experience.

One of the first lectures I did for the Forest Service, I wasn't sure of the receptivity of my audience. Minutes into the talk I noticed a shift in my audience. They were sitting up and attentive. They were listening and sharing. They shared through words, body language, and through their emotions. Their stories touched, inspired, and moved me. An occasional person sat with their arms crossed and seemed less than impressed. Even those students were guiding and teaching me.

I want to share with you a true story and the lesson I learned from a man in the front row. We'll call him Steve. Steve was a leadership manager for the Forest Service. He taught leadership skills to his team of potential managers and supervisors. I stood in front of Steve and the other students, talking about a little boy that worked for me cleaning stalls.

I described this young man and his quiet and shy nature. I described his body language; shoulders slumped, eyes cast down, lips tight with no sign of a smile. Tim was only twelve and small for his age. I gestured his height with my hand as I continued on with my story. I told how each day I made a point to say greet Tim and tell him I appreciated his hard work. I told how, for months, I followed this routine of acknowledging Tim and his good work. Tim never said a word; he simply nodded and looked away.

One day I noticed Tim always spoke to the horses. He carried on conversations and hummed a tune as he worked in and around my animals. The horses liked him. Tim was quiet and kind, and moved slowly and deliberately, around them. He made my horses feel safe.

It was six months before Tim would acknowledge me and return my greeting. I noticed, when I spoke to Tim about the horses, he listened a bit more closely. I told him how much I appreciated his kindness to my horses and mentioned they seemed to really like him. I began to see a slight smile on Tim's face soon after that.

I also gave Tim an added chore of grooming a few of my horses and turning them out into the pasture. I taught Tim how to cue horses to lower their heads so they could be haltered. (A big help when you are only 4'8"!) Tim stopped by to greet me as he hummed a tune on the way to the barn from then on. He shared tidbits about some of the horses and their antics as he turned them out in to the pasture.

Tim stayed with me for several years. He grew into a fine young horseman and went on to college where he graduated as a grade school teacher. This story is about the impact we can have on others in this world, how we can choose to guide others in a positive way when we honor them as individuals and take the time to learn about what is important to them. It's through this patient observation we open doors for others and positively impact them. Being a leader is not about making others do what we see as important. A leader helps others grow into their strengths. Sometimes that means helping them find their voice.

Remember, I mentioned Steve in the front row, the leadership supervisor? At the end of the talk I opened the session up for discussion. I felt proud of myself for a job well done.

Steve spoke up. "I have a question. When you gestured with your hand Tim's height, your hand signaled to a smaller height than your own. Is that because you feel superior to Tim, and that he was smaller not only in size, but in his work position at your barn?"

Wow, seriously, this was what caught this man's attention. I was floored. I nicely stated, "No, that wasn't my intention at all. Tim was a little boy. I was trying to give everyone a picture before I went too far into the story of what Tim was like, etc."

That moment has never left me. Steve taught me a valuable lesson. I realized we are all in a different place mentally, emotionally, and spiritually. I believe we can all learn something from that story, or from any story, each of us with all our uniqueness will take away what is important at that time. For me it was the lesson not everyone is at the same stage of openness and learning. Instead, we're on our own path. Steve was stuck on the aspect of judging others and sometimes using metaphors or gestures to label people.

Did Steve completely read me wrong or was he trying to find fault in my lecture and missed the essence of the story? Was he projecting his guilt of labeling others in the workplace? I guess we'll never know as my job that day wasn't to dig deeper into Steve's question, but to share ideas and insight into how we lead and guide others. Remember we can find ourselves, at any moment, student or teacher.

CHAPTER 20

IMAGINATION

The definition of imagination is the ability to form images and ideas in the mind, especially of things never seen or experienced directly. When you imagine or dream anything is possible. We live in a time of high tech video games and movies. Children spend hours and hours playing these games and are entertained by someone else who is doing the imagining for them.

I grew up in a rural area so playing by myself was what I knew. I'd go outside and play horse show for hours. Sometimes I'd be the judge and imagine a ring full of horses ridden by various types of riders. I'd judge and then place them accordingly. I also played the role of rider and walked, jogged, and loped around my imaginary arena. I visualized arena obstacles in my mind so I could pretend showing in a trail class. Sometimes I placed and sometimes I didn't. I experienced beauty in the moment by simply imagining it.

I often found myself daydreaming in school. (I know I should have paid better attention to my teacher, but I daydreamed a lot!) My childhood best friend, Pam, and I created our own world. We had such vivid imaginations. One summer day I was at Pam's house. We decided we'd rather watch TV than play outside. Before the TV was even turned on Pam's mother directed us right back out the door to play. At the time we wondered why it was such a big deal?

Thank you so much, Mrs. Welch, for teaching us to play, dream, and explore instead of sitting and letting someone else do the imagining for us.

I also spent hours imagining I lived in a log home out in the country. I imagined a long gravel drive, my horses pastured on either side, so I'd see them as I drove home. My dream grew through the years to include an indoor arena and what my life would be like in this wonderful paradise I held close in my thoughts.

Forty years later, I live in a wonderful log home with a gravel driveway where my horses are pastured as I drive in. I have an indoor arena and I love showing my horses. Because I used my imagination in a positive way, I'm a much more confident and secure person. I continue to dream and imagine the wonderful possibilities for my future.

We often encourage our children to use their imagination, to be creative and to believe they can be and do anything. As we get older, we seem too busy to daydream. As adults we're told its okay to be imaginative, in a practical sense, but somehow we limit this gift of dreaming if it appears to be impossible or unrealistic.

I have learned how powerful our minds are and that being able to dream and create our destiny is a gift. A developed and strong imagination does not make you a daydreamer and impractical. On the contrary, it strengthens your creative abilities. Daydreaming is a great tool for recreating and remodeling your world.

I challenge you to do two things: Go back to your childhood days, relive the things you once dreamed. Then give yourself permission to imagine anything and everything you'd like to experience for at least five minutes a day. Consider this your time to relax, dream, and believe. Only you know the dreams and goals you hold dear. Why not spend some time creating the experience in your mind? You may be surprised by how much future success is inspired by it.

CHAPTER 21

INTEGRITY

Integrity means doing what is right whether you are alone or in a group; doing the right thing no matter what the rewards or consequences may be. Integrity means putting your base of beliefs into action.

It takes strength of character to have integrity. Imagine yourself in a group of five people. One of the five urges the group into something you know is not right. Peer pressure is a powerful thing and people do things they would normally not consider. However, by saying no, you may provide the strength for others to say no. Take a stand for something you believe in, it feels good to honor not only the situation and yourself. Integrity is doing what you know is right, regardless.

Let me share a story about Bill. He's thoughtful, intelligent, inquisitive, adventurous, and he has integrity. I met him in 2007 while skiing in the mountains of Montana. We took a chair lift together and visited. We shared a few runs together followed by an exchange of e-mails.

Bill is a single dad (then with a fifteen-year-old daughter). He shared custody so she spent every two weeks with her dad and then would alternate to her mother's home. Bill is a loving devoted father. We fell head over heels for one another. Bill was careful to take it slow when it came to my relationship with his daughter. It was important that his daughter felt safe and secure in her world.

I considered myself a pretty safe and caring person, so I was a bit taken back when Bill shared the promise he'd made to his daughter. Bill promised her that he would not remarry until she was out of high school. His daughter had already gone through the throes of a divorce, and her Mother had remarried. Her world turned upside down. Bill was determined that he would be her safe place in a not always so safe world.

We lived fifty miles apart. Deeply in love and committed to one another, it'd be four and a half years of commuting and coordinating our schedules to spend time with one another. There were times I didn't think I'd be able to wait for this relationship to go to the next level.

There was no doubt that Bill loved me. Two years into the relationship he took me flying over the Mission Mountains and proposed. Knowing full well we had another two years before we would walk down the aisle, I said yes.

Some people criticized Bill for making me wait. His family wanted Bill to marry me and felt it was wrong for him to ask me to wait. His daughter also told her dad, "Just get married, Dad. I'm fine with it." Bill had made a promise, a commitment, and although in many ways it would have been easier to give in, and get married, Bill is a man of great integrity.

We were married August 27th, 2011. Surrounded by family and friends.

Was it a tough four years? Sometimes. Would I change one minute of it? No, I wouldn't. Bill stood for something he believed in. When loved ones criticized and pressured for something different, he stood by his word. He wanted his daughter to know you honor a commitment, not just when it's easy and convenient, but in the hard and uncomfortable times. What a beautiful gift to give to his daughter.

Integrity is a character trait that tells a story of who we are. Remember that we are all a work in progress. Our journey is ever evolving. With each new day we're given the opportunity to become a better person. I have been given the gift of a man who taught me what integrity really means.

CHAPTER 22

LABELS

Labels are words we assign to a person that describes the characteristics we believe stand out the most in someone's personality, position, looks, or demeanor. Labels can be positive or negative. Words like fun, energetic, outgoing, shy, manipulative, grouchy, lazy and so on. In our society, we tend to label our spouses, children, co-workers, and everyone in-between.

I've discovered we not only do this to people, but we also do this to our animals. As a horse trainer I'm amazed at the labels owners will put on their horse. Words like aggressive, stupid, spooky, and lazy are a few common ones.

In my work with the Forest Service on leadership and the subtleties of body language, I came up with an example of the effect labels can have on horses and humans. The scenario goes something like this: I ask four people to help me with my labeling exercise. Each person holds a sign up with a common label used to describe a horse. I usually use the words, aggressive, lazy, spooky, and average. I show a short skit of what I encounter with each label when someone brings me a horse to train. I take the part of the owner.

For the aggressive horse I describe the horse as easily agitated, he will bite, kick and is pushy but notice I assign emotional words. My body language is clearly defensive and harsh as I stand next to the aggressive horse. I act anxious and easily angered as I describe my horse's characteristics.

Then I move on to the lazy horse and speak slowly. I stop often to gather my thoughts. I use words and body language such as, "He just doesn't seem to want to learn," or "He's hard to motivate."

The next horse is the spooky one. "She's nervous, and jumpy, every little thing sets her off." My body language is quick and edgy, often moving and unsettled. My voice, fast and tense.

The last label is average. This horse is described as a great horse, willing and happy, with tons of talent. My tone of voice is even and happy. I show signs of confidence and poise.

The actual word or label is not the problem; the problem lies in the energy and emotion we assign. *Remember, your horse is a mirror image of you.* As a trainer I want to know if a horse has aggressive tendencies. I want to know if a horse is spooky. But I do not want to give emotion and life to those words. Of course safety is crucial, but if I give those labels energy and emotion, I will create the very thing I want to change.

So let's go back to our spouses, our children, friends, and co-workers. Maybe they are lazy or intense. The question is: how do we cope in a positive manner that allows the person to grow and excel? First, we must be acutely aware to avoid negative labels and not fuel them with emotional energy, but instead use the energy to be constructive. If you tell a horse often enough, through your body language and tone of voice, that he's aggressive, he'll only get worse. We've focused solely on the problem area and we will mirror the problem back to the horse. We can redirect this energy, and send the message, "You're doing a good job." Then reward a positive behavior. Wonderful changes happen.

Is that not also true of humans? Remember, change does not happen overnight but builds over time by positive reinforcement. Note we not only label others, but we label ourselves as well. We must be careful of the words we use to describe ourselves just as much as we need to be aware of the words we use to describe others.

My horses have given me such wonderful gifts, teaching me so many valuable life lessons. Fifteen years ago I had no idea the lessons I learn as a professional horse trainer and clinician fold over to so many different areas of my life. The lessons I've learned about labeling are invaluable. Labeling is only as powerful as the emotion and energy you give it. So learn to be cautious of those labels you wish to understand and change. And to embrace the positive labels you want to grow in.

CHAPTER 23

LEARNING

We are all students of life. We should never stop learning, reaching, and growing. No matter who you are, each day offers us an opportunity to grow.

As a teacher I've become acutely aware of life's daily lessons. In my work with horses, one of the biggest lessons I try to instill in my students is awareness. Through awareness comes knowledge and insight. Awareness means learning to listen. Listening to your inner voice, listening to what your horse says through his body language, listening to others and what they have to offer. Listening is the art of learning.

We learn from everyone and everything. We learn from our parents, siblings, and friends. We learn from our teachers and mentors. We learn from our experiences in life. We learn from our horses, dogs, and from nature—if we're aware and hear what's being said. Listening happens in many different forms. It can certainly be to hear what someone is saying but it goes much deeper than that. To listen is to understand body language, the subtleties of tones of voice, from gestures and mannerisms, eye contact, facial expression—all of this teaches us to become more aware and to appreciate what others have to offer.

For the leadership workshop at the local college, when I presented, "Actions Speak Louder Than Words" I wondered what

I could to say to a group of corporate people about leadership. I'm a horse trainer. I realized the lessons my horses taught me through the years were invaluable. Horses have a way of teaching us to still our minds and stay present. They teach us about fairness and justice. They teach us how to quiet our minds so that we are more tuned in to the small things.

In my opening presentation, I talked to the participants about how they'd been watching me as I prepared for my lecture. People take mental notes that help them decide how they feel about a person. These impressions determine if they'll like me, and felt intrigued, or if they disliked me and dismissed me before I spoke. These decisions were being made by many different factors for my audience. Were my speech patterns and body language appealing? Did I look confident and friendly or cocky and stern? They also made judgments based on my attire. It's human nature; we all are guilty of passing judgment on first impressions.

Then I posed a question. "Are you aware of the messages you were sending me during this time?" Some had their arms crossed and looked defensive. Others tried not to appear to be watching, but obviously were curious about the speaker. Some were simply engaged with colleagues and paid no attention. It's always an interesting opening because most people are so busy sizing up someone else they often forget about their not so silent messages. Learning to be aware of our actions, we have better control of what we want to project. We learn to not judge so quickly.

Horses do the very same thing, but with one major difference. They never forget the message sent to another horse. Horses are hyper aware of who they are and what they are projecting. If you ever watch horses in a pasture, you will notice that when a new horse is introduced they will all pay very close attention to whether the new horse is nervous, aggressive, or dominant all while checking their position within their own herd.

I'm amazed at what I learn each time I present one of my leadership lectures. People are wonderful and fun and creative. Others offer so much if we're willing to let out guard down enough to hear them and weigh what they have to offer.

An interesting thing happened recently while flying back to Connecticut from Montana. It's a fairly long flight. I hoped to have a few hours of quiet time to work on material I'd be presenting to a new client. An elderly gentleman sat next to me. He wanted to visit and no matter how hard I tried to be polite and gently demonstrate I had work to do, he just kept on talking. I tried everything, from closing my eyes to reading my work material. He just kept right on talking.

I had a change of planes in Minneapolis and was relieved when I finally was reseated on the next flight. Well, as fate would have it, a well-known horse trainer was seated right next to me. Excited to have this person next to me, I decided to start a conversation. All of a sudden my work seemed unimportant. This person wasn't friendly and made it very clear he did not want to be bothered. A light bulb went off. How rude of me to not find the importance of the elderly gentleman, yet I wanted to engage with someone who shared a common bond.

I wondered what lessons I missed by not engaging more with that older gentleman. Sometimes we dismiss people who we don't think can be beneficial to us. It's a never-ending lesson. Everyone has value. Everyone has a story—if only we're willing to listen.

CHAPTER 24

MOTIVATION

Motivation is the desire to reach one's goals. *Motivation* is defined as the process that initiates, guides, and maintains goal-oriented behaviors. Motivation is what causes us to act, whether to get a glass of water to reduce thirst or reading a book to gain knowledge.

Different types of motivation are frequently described as being either extrinsic or intrinsic. Extrinsic motivations are those that arise from outside of the individual and often involve rewards such as trophies, money, social recognition, or praise. Intrinsic motivations are those that arise from within the individual, such as doing a complicated crossword puzzle purely for the personal gratification of solving a problem. My goal is to help my students learn intrinsic motivation. Learn to love the battle, and what they can become, rather than what they can receive.

There isn't a road map for teaching someone about motivation. There isn't one formula that fits every scenario. Motivation is personal. I believe motivation is taught through timing and feel. If motivation is taught by timing and feel, many elements must be in place before the motivation can begin. Things like focus, confidence, trust, and faith. Those elements can also be a byproduct received from others as lessons.

I understand people are highly motivated and successful with minimal help along the way. But I also believe sharing our journey with others is how we find the most meaning in our lives.

I teach an apprenticeship class on self-development and training horses. The very first thing I ask my students to do is to write about their dreams. The following is a piece of the first assignment I give to my students in the Apprenticeship Program.

> The importance of dreaming and setting goals cannot be over-emphasized. Without a dream and goals, people tend to wander aimlessly letting external circumstances guide them. A couple of simple tools to help you get started:

> When we were young, our imaginations soared. We didn't need much to spark our enthusiasm to dream about what we wanted to achieve with our horses (or what you'd do with a horse someday). As we grew, so did our dreams and interests. School, careers, marriage and family took priority and, for many of us, our horse dreams and goals were put on hold.

> Too often, those "priorities" caused us to live in a "comfort zone" and sometimes to be afraid to "step out of the box" or explore new things and dream new dreams.

> Goals all start with a dream—but here's the tough part: You've got to write it down. Dreaming can inspire you in many ways. The beauty of dreaming is that you are only limited by your imagination. If you want to dream, all you need is a creative mind and willingness to fantasize. However, to turn a dream into a reality, you need much more. You need a set of goals and a plan. It's only the set of goals, together with a plan, that can effectively be pursued and achieved. Think of this assignment as beginning a journey to

becoming the horseperson you've dreamed about. The fulfillment of your dream begins here.

Find a quiet and comfortable place. Write a description of the ultimate horseperson you'd like to be. In your writing, don't hold back—the sky is the limit! Go ahead. Take out a magic wand. Use words like: graceful, elegant, controlled, assertive, physically fit, having fun! Go for it! Take your time.

I've found is this assignment can be difficult for many of my students. Somewhere along the way they have forgotten how to dream, how to motivate themselves, and believe that they can achieve their goals.

As a teacher it's my job to help open that door. I want to inspire my students to regain their passion. There is time spent working on the fundamentals (like writing out their dreams) but there's also time spent talking, laughing, sharing stories and learning about one another to build a relationship outside of the Apprenticeship Program.

People communicate in different ways if you are tuned in and learn to listen. A leader's job is to learn to read an individual as an individual, different from others, unique in their own way. One student may verbally say, "Kathy I'm really feeling down right now and unmotivated to ride my horse." Another student may say the very same thing but communicate through facial expressions and body language. There are countless different ways to communicate. A good leader learns to respond to each.

One of the most fascinating things about leading is deciphering how different people communicate. I improve as an instructor when I learn to respond in a quicker and more effective manner. I get better by continually learning and reaching and being motivated to do better, be better, and to give fully.

This is where the timing and "feel" come into play. With horses communication is all about reading body language. Great timing means learning how to be ahead of your horse; help him before he gets himself into too much trouble. Then learning how to feel the right level of pressure so that the learning experience is a positive one for the horse. This is true in people as well. Once you understand individuality, then you realize everyone is motivated differently. There is no one size fits all formula. I motivate both horses and people by feel. With people there are times for a pat on the back, a time for a smile or a nod for a job well done. There are times for being tough and direct about what needs to be done. Motivating people must be a flexible and versatile process. Create history with people if you are going to coach or lead them. It's through history trust emerges. It's through trust change happens.

A student worked with me as an assistant trainer. Her name is Shannon. She decided to show at one of the local shows. She made a huge mistake before entering her class by putting an unfamiliar bit in her horse's mouth. Her horse was uncomfortable with the change and distracted by the new bit. Long story short, it wasn't a pretty picture in the show pen. The following day a woman who knows this young girl and who fancies herself as a horseman called my assistant and told her in no uncertain terms that she had watched the show and the performance was horrible. She criticized my assistant's skills and told her she should find a new instructor. Shannon was in tears and felt she had not only let herself down, but me as well.

I wasn't aware on the day of the show about the use of a different bit. Shannon and I had a long conversation about the impact of what she had done and what she learned from the situation. Life is about learning and Shannon learned an important lesson, one she will never repeat, but also a good experience, given her desire to become a professional horse trainer.

I was tough on my assistant about what had happened, but I'd built a relationship with her. We have history. So although my criticism was tough, she could learn because of understanding that I care. The woman who called came from a place of anger and had no history built. Therefore, my assistant could only hear the anger and meanness in this woman's voice. Shannon was highly motivated to do better in the future and vowed to treat others with dignity and respect, especially when coaching or teaching her students.

I follow my heart in these situations. I instinctively react to the needs of my horses and my students. Even as a teacher and leader, I don't always take on the leader role. There are times I let others take the lead. One of my assistant trainers or a student may say or do something that benefits their classmates more than I can. Sometimes a student will share and everyone benefits. No one person can be the only source of learning and motivation. There is something special about the camaraderie that happens with my students; their belief, excitement, and commitment to each other is powerful.

Motivation comes from building relationships that nurture one another and from a safe place to learn and grow. Do you have people in your life that can help you grow and succeed in whatever passions you may have? Or, more importantly, are you someone others see as a leader? Do you offer a safe place to learn and share hopes and dreams with, someone who motivates and encourages all that they can be? This is what motivates me to be a better leader. When we motivate one another the journey is just that much sweeter!

CHAPTER 25

OPPORTUNITY

Life is filled with opportunities. Sometimes they are placed within easy grasp, other times they seem far out of reach. Opportunities are all around us each and every day if we are willing to pay attention and take advantage of them.

Does everyone but you seem to get ahead? Opportunities just don't to come your way? I understand that train of thought because I've been there. It seemed like I was never at the right place at the right time. When I began working with horses I found a new perspective on what it means to seize an opportunity.

I took a horse training certification program in Parachute, Colorado, to hone my training skills. I was on a colt I'd only ridden a few times when a windstorm kicked up and the dust began to blow.

The instructor said, "I see you're thinking about getting off that colt. What a shame. Training opportunities like this don't happen every day."

It was a light-bulb moment. I wanted to give my colt the gift of trust and confidence, and I almost blew it. How would he ever be able to learn how to handle this kind of situation if I didn't give him a chance? Keep in mind I knew I had enough rides on this colt to help him through a scary situation and we were in the safety of an arena. He jumped a little but it was a fantastic opportunity to teach him to respond to his cues in a new situation. I taught him to trust in me when things became frightening.

I've used this philosophy almost daily with my students. A dog running around the horses, the bike going by, a loose tarp on the hay pile are all opportunities to teach and learn, given the right set of circumstances. You see if we do not learn to practice our skills from all the opportunities that present themselves then there's no way we'll be ready when we really need it. If we are not practicing, you cannot expect a skill to be pulled out of nowhere. As I practice with my horses, I get better at my horsemanship skills and my horses get better at the trust and confidence they need and deserve to be safe, fun, and talented performance horses.

I take everything I say to heart. If I'm going to teach it then I must also abide by it. When I lived in Connecticut one of my neighbors was angry because the road we live on was gravel and created dust. I lived on a gravel road because I chose to. My home was three hundred feet off the road and a little dust did not bother me in the least. My neighbors bought a home twenty feet off the gravel road. They were less than pleasant when they approached me about oiling the road. There are many reasons I don't like oil. On a rainy day, it's a muddy, slick mess, not to mention less than enjoyable to walk my dog on or ride my horses down. However before I could greet them, they were madder than a wet cat telling me I had to pay for oil. I disagreed. They became angry over anything and everything I did.

At first I felt angry too. I've lived in my home without issue far longer than they had and how dare they be so rude to me. A pancake, no matter how flat you make it, has two sides. So this is my side. Then it hit me. This is a golden opportunity to work on my leadership skills. I called and set up a meeting with them at their home. On their turf, they'd feel less threatened. Hopefully my offer to meet with them would be a sign of a good neighbor gesture.

"Just what is it you want to discuss?" they asked.

I said, "Me."

I met with them later that week. Both defensive and angry, their body language was firm and cold with arms crossed, standing, not sitting.

I told them that I was sorry if I'd been difficult and I wanted us to be good neighbors.

The woman glared at me and said, "Well, Kathy, you have been very difficult."

Honestly, jumping up and having a few choice words to say to her did cross my mind for a millisecond. Then I said in a quiet and calm voice, "Yes I have and I'm sorry. Can we move forward in our relationship as neighbors?"

She walked over and hugged me. I had managed to diffuse the situation and create the beginning of a solution to our issues.

I sleep well knowing I'm doing my best to seize every opportunity life gives me so I can grow and succeed.

There are opportunities everywhere; the bank, park, on the job, with our horses, and our children. If we want to get better, and do better, in our lives we can't just wait for the big moment. We must work at these skills daily. When the really important occasion arises we'll have the gift of knowledge from years of honing our life skills to be better people, better horseman, and better leaders. Opportunities await you. Will you seize the moment?

CHAPTER 26

Passion

When you love what you're doing, pursuing something that drives you from deep in your soul, that's passion. Passion is creative, strong, and unyielding. People with passion burn with a desire to move forward and are excited to grow and learn. What are you passionate about?

I have been fortunate to do many things I'm passionate about. Before I pursued my career in the equine world as a professional, I drove a catering truck to construction sites and businesses. I served breakfast and lunch. It was a high-pressure job servicing a large number of businesses in a small amount of time. So being quick and efficient was important. The job required me to stock the truck at 4:00 a.m. Winter service happened outside, in 10 degrees with a wind chill of below 40.

I hated my job at first. I mentally fought every aspect of it. *I should be doing something better than this. I deserve better.* Then I began to look forward to seeing my customers. Since I've always had a competitive spirit, I'd challenge myself to be the top seller of the week in a fleet of eight trucks and drivers. What a great way to learn people skills and how to work under intense pressure.

My next career was as a long haul truck driver. I drove for Allied Van Lines in their long-haul fleet as an owner operator. This involved loading and unloading people's household goods and driving across the country. Moving is a stressful time for most people. They may be faced with a career change, leaving family and friends, and sometimes leaving a home they truly love. As a mover, the furniture is someone's history, family heirlooms, and precious pieces that tell their story. At first I had no appreciation for any of this. It was a job. Move this from point *A* to point *B* and be done. Wow, was I ever in for a rude awakening!

People were sometimes angry or sad or agitated. They'd sometimes lash out at me and could be very demanding. I needed to quit or figure out how to do a better job. Once I made a mental switch, to learn and excel, everything changed. It was awesome. I was excited to travel and learn about people and new places. Because of that career I learned leadership and business skills and also acquired a lot of good old-fashioned common sense rules. I learned about equipment maintenance for diesel trucks and trailers, how to pull a fifty-foot trailer and negotiate tight places (invaluable when I pull my horse trailer), and how to read a road map. (I know, I know we have Google maps now but I still love to read a map!)

I was passionate about the process. I didn't grow up saying, "Gee, I want to be a long haul truck driver." I first had dreams of being a veterinarian, then I thought I wanted to own a boarding stable. Later I realized I wanted to be a professional horse trainer and travel across the country teaching clinics. I never dreamed I would run a successful apprenticeship program and become a public speaker on leadership.

I was passionate about whatever life gave me—and still am to this day. If I had not learned such a wide variety of lessons, I'm not sure I'd be as successful in my current career. I can see how much everything I do now is a reflection of what I accomplished years earlier.

Sometimes it's difficult to work toward your passion because of the roadblocks that you may face. The fear of failure looms over you. Remember the chapter on opportunities—life is filled with opportunities. I love this quote, "Nothing in life happens to us. It happens for us." So whatever you are facing, or have faced, it's an opportunity for growth and an opportunity to move forward into your passion.

My mother grew up poor, married an abusive husband, had four children, and was stuck in a very unhappy life. But being a strong and compassionate woman, she learned from those difficult situations. She went back to school and became a nurse's aid. She was passionate about helping others. Mom loved being independent and self-sufficient. My mother had many passions in her life, from her children to her home to her career. She was also a passionate and talented horsewoman. Not all of us are born into the perfect life. It's what we do with that life that's important.

My hope is you're thinking, *Wow, I'm passionate about* _____, Fill in the blank. If you feel like you have no passion, and life is overwhelming, then I hope you will consider taking charge of those thoughts and creating a vision for yourself that excites you. Sometimes we just have to seize the moment and life will take us in a new and magnificent direction. This can be a wonderful adventure if we're open to the possibilities that present themselves to us.

CHAPTER 27

SELFLESS

Selfless may refer to: Selflessness, the act of sacrificing one's own interest for the greater good. People who are selfless have the ability to give to others without the need to be in the spotlight or acknowledged for doing something good for others. For those who are selfless, it's enough for them to know they shared something relevant in their lives.

I've been criticized for my generosity in giving to others, especially in my business. It seems I should be charging more and giving less. Although sometimes true, I enjoy being able to help others have the opportunity to learn something new about themselves or their horses. Sure, I need to make a living. But I also need to live a full life. I've never had a sleepless night because I hadn't given 110%. I prefer being thought of as generous and caring rather than selfless. Funny we have a personal way to describe ourselves!

I was blessed to know and to be friends with Janie. She was the poster child for selflessness and generosity. Janie and I met in 2001, the year I moved to the Bitterroot Valley in Montana. She and her husband Brooke were the first people who opened their doors and welcomed me. Janie loved life, she loved Montana, and she loved her horses. I'm going to share a little piece of my journey with

Janie—the friendship and horse part of our connection. There's so much more to Janie's story but that just might be another book!

Janie grew up in an abusive family environment. She lost her mother at an early age and her father made it clear she'd never amount to anything. Janie's grandparents took her in and nurtured her. Through their love and care, Janie persevered and went on to college to become a social scientist.

Janie owned two mares when we met, Cody and Simone. Janie's mares had issues that needed to be managed. Janie decided to immerse herself in learning all she could about herself and horse training to be a great horse owner for Cody and Simone. I don't believe I've had a client/friend who gave so much when it came to her loyalty and sacrifice to her friends, husband, and her horses.

Janie spent an entire summer with me learning and developing her skills and understanding of horses. She lit up when we'd get together to talk about her horses' progress. She would talk so fast and so full of excitement it was hard to keep up. Her enthusiasm was contagious. She'd have a big smile, and her arms and hands waved, in an effort to show me all she learned and discovered. Eager for more, she'd put in long hours at work so she could afford to continue this journey of discovery.

Cody and Simone bloomed. The changes were amazing. Both mares became quiet and relaxed; they would look to Janie for direction. A bond of trust and respect had been formed.

Janie would talk to anyone who would listen about learning better ways to communicate with her animals. Janie did not care about driving a fancy truck or owning designer clothes. She was authentic. Janie was deep, spiritually and emotionally. If you did not know her very well Janie could come across as irritating, stubborn, and hardheaded. She was determined to make a difference in this world. Janie was also unbelievably loyal, kind, and loving.

I remember one winter she gave me a Christmas gift to go cross-country skiing with her. We laughed, we fell, we told stories, and we took in the beauty of a perfect Montana winter day in the mountains. Janie wanted me to experience the beauty and awe of being outside on a mountaintop and connecting with one's soul.

She always looked out for me though she had so many things going on in her own life. Janie offered me strength and courage, love and support, when my mother was dying of cancer. Janie was diagnosed with stage-four lymphoma, yet she still managed to be there for me in my struggles.

Janie gave me strength and guidance in moments of uncertainty about my chosen career path. She was my biggest fan. Janie was sure I could make a difference in the horse world. She felt so strongly God's creatures needed a voice. Janie was sure I was that voice. Janie's work involved editing. She offered anything I needed to make a book happen.

Summer of 2006, Janie's lymphoma reared its ugly head. Devastating as this was, Janie moved forward, learning and reaching out to others as she faced the toughest journey in her life. Her horses remained the rock Janie needed when life was too overwhelming. She rode no matter the weather and often called me to talk training and share stories of her precious horses. I would sit with Janie during her chemotherapy and she would delight in my tales of horses and people as we held hands. One might say I was a good friend, but it was Janie who was the good one. She shared with me a very intimate part of her life. Her fears, sorrows, and joys.

In December of 2010, Janie was rushed into the hospital where they discovered leukemia. My dear friend had two weeks to live. I will never forget this time with my friend. In her hospital bed, her concerns were for her husband, animals, and friends. She never forgot to thank the nurses and doctors for even the smallest assist. She would whisper a thank you to every friend that came to visit. She worried about her dog, Hansie, and her horses. A dear friend brought Janie a beautiful photo album with 8 x 10s of all her animals. Then they snuck in her dog by putting a service dog vest on her! They brought Hansie right through the hospital's main entrance, up the elevator, and into Janie's room! They put a sheet on the bed so her dog could curl up next to her! She was deeply loved by many.

I remember when she asked me to sit with her so she could get some rest. She told me that so many dear friends were stopping by and she felt the need to entertain them! Can you imagine, Janie still worried about others in the last days of her life? She told me I brought a sense of peace to her. One of the kindest things anyone has ever said to me. Later in the day, she asked me to help her with a bath. I will never forget how tenderly she touched my face. "You are my sister, thank you."

Janie passed away two days later.

Janie simply gave and gave and gave even in her darkest hours. She gave me treasured gifts; the gifts of love, loyalty, and compassion. A sad story, but I felt the need to share because life is short and precious. We need to be reminded sometimes the important stuff of life isn't always what we need or want, but what we give. Janie my friend, I wrote the book and I'm forever grateful of your love and selflessness.

CHAPTER 28

STRATEGY

To have a strategy one must have a plan of action. Strategy is a tactic or blueprint for how to complete a task.

I like to think I'm a person who uses strategy and works hard at accomplishing difficult tasks. I've always taken pride in this characteristic until I met a man who showed me what strategy and determination really means. Lou paid me a visit on a warm spring day in 2010. Six feet, he carried himself with poise and confidence. He's a handsome older man with a deep voice and a lot of charm.

Lou shared that his daughters had horses and competed with them many years prior. He, however, had some unpleasant experiences such as horses running off and bucking. He felt fear when he thought about riding. Lou was embarrassed he was a big tough guy, retired from the police force, and he was afraid of horses. He now had grandchildren who are avid riders. Lou wanted to surprise them with the ability to go for a trail ride with them on his next visit. Lou had a plan. This man had thought through what he needed to accomplish. He asked me if I could help him accomplish this goal.

Lou took weekly lessons using my personal horse, Jag. We began with the basics: learning how to approach a horse in his stall, halter him, then on to leading, tying, grooming, and saddling. Then on to riding and negotiating obstacles he might encounter on a trail. The end of our strategy included loading horses and taking a trail ride in the beautiful Bitterroot Mountains.

On our first day Lou showed up at the barn feeling a bit nervous. We stayed with our plan to help Lou get comfortable with horses. I had no idea how much fear this man had until I opened up the stall door. As I explained to Lou what we were going to do, I noted he was now five feet away from the stall door, listening. Lou's fears were alive and well and we would have to work diligently to overcome them.

Little by little I began to see the changes in Lou. He was now showing up for his lessons twenty minutes early to brush and saddle Jag before our lesson. His wore big grin when he told me Jag met him at the door ready to go.

"He likes me!" He said with a childlike enthusiasm. We all should have that kind of excitement and passion in our lives.

"Yes, he does like you Lou!"

As the months went by, Lou had begun to transform from passenger to rider. I watched as he took control when Jag tested Lou's authority. I set up obstacles for Lou and Jag to negotiate. From bridges to cross to poles to step over, and even some difficult formations to back through, Lou and Jag shined. We had our tough days too. Sometimes Jag and Lou were not in synch. Bless both their hearts, I never heard a complaint. I saw determination and true grit in both of them. As time went on Lou and I developed a wonderful relationship. I always rode another horse when giving lessons to Lou. It allowed me to demonstrate different techniques like how to move a horse through or around different obstacles. Lou also learned how to negotiate riding with other people. We joked and shared bits of our lives while riding. We enjoyed the amazing journey that Lou decided to take on.

Finally, the big day arrived for Lou and I to hit the trails. Lou showed up and stated, "I'm brave enough to do this trail ride only because I trust you and Jag."

We arrived at the trailhead at 10:00 a.m. and unloaded our horses. When we headed down the first leg of our trek, Lou looked a bit nervous. He held the reins in one hand and the horn in the other. He was very quiet which I had learned wasn't in his character! Within a half hour, Lou was relaxed again. We crossed water, bridges, downed trees and rocks. We rode for almost two hours. At one point Lou took the reins in one hand and his phone in another and checked messages. Talk about relaxed! Lou was smiling from ear to ear. Jag was a testimonial to Lou's relaxation as he walked along quietly, head low, listening to every cue his rider gave him.

I felt an enormous sense of pride in Lou. He'd conquered his fears and stuck to his strategy. Lesson by lesson, week by week, Lou became more accomplished in his riding. He was excited to share all he had learned with his grandchildren.

When Lou returned from his trip he told me he wanted to continue lessons but now his goal had changed. Lou wanted to compete in Western Trail on my mare Fancy. She's a very talented mare, but also a more temperamental horse than Jag. He had a new strategy on how to reach this goal. Lou rode twice a week to prepare for a show.

Do you wonder what Lou's current status is on this last endeavor? I recently held a showing Western Trail Workshop with six riders who rode with me for two days. The final day I set up the trail course. The students judged one another as they ran the pattern to learn what a judge looks for, and it also puts a bit of pressure on them as they rode. When it was Lou's turn to go he sat up tall in the saddle and eyed the course. I knew he was strategizing of how he would approach and exit each obstacle. He nailed every maneuver. Over the bridge, across raised poles, side passing a difficult pattern and backing through a *doglegged "L"*. He was a man on a mission. He stayed calm and cool and quiet with his horse. Because of Lou, Fancy felt confident and free to do her job. The two of them melded. As they completed the course, the other students applauded. What a perfect run! Lou won the class. Not bad for a man who, not that long ago, came to me with a vision and a plan to ride a horse, at a walk, down a trail with his grandchildren.

Lou taught me some valuable lessons. I'm grateful for the lessons and even more grateful for our friendship.

I hope you have a plan of action. It's never too late. We are never too old. Life is exciting and filled with wonder. All it takes is a desire and a bit of strategic planning.

CHAPTER 29

STRESS

Stress, as described in the dictionary: mental, emotional, or physical strain caused by anxiety or overwork. Stress may cause symptoms like raised blood pressure or depression. Just reading or even hearing the word *stress* can cause some people to feel anxious.

We live in a society where stress is a big topic. There is stress at every turn. I believe we have been programmed to think of stress as a bad thing, something to avoid. People go to the doctor for an illness only to have the doctor say they need to get rid of the stress. *No kidding but that is next to impossible.* The message is that stress is a bad thing. Sometimes I feel like our society has gone to extremes to avoid stress. We have drugs to relax us and we give ourselves permission to avoid stressful situations. I disagree with eliminating all stress. Stress is, and always will be, a part of our lives. We need to learn how to cope and stay mentally strong if we are going to live a full, happy, and productive life.

The key in my opinion is to not avoid stress but instead to see a new perspective. If you look at it as an opportunity to develop better coping skills, then stress can be welcomed. We shouldn't live in a stressful environment all the time. Stress without recovery can be deadly. We do need time to relax and feel peace from time to time. However, many times we simply need moments, yes moments, to regroup—not hours or days.

I seemed to have a more difficult time with this chapter than any other. Then by chance (or was it?) I happened to be preparing for a leadership lecture about how leaders must feel pain. We often avoid feeling emotions. Instead we lead with our brains and not our hearts. The reason I'm good at what I do is because I have the ability to feel emotion. I'm not afraid of emotion. I actually embrace it. Now I'm not talking about huggy-feely babble. I'm talking about my ability to embrace both positive and negative emotions. That's my point about stress; stress causes us to grow as humans. We get stronger, more resilient, confidant, and creative. Stress is a good thing, a great thing, if we face it with the right attitude. It's about allowing oneself to feel the emotions we spend so much of our lives avoiding, like the pain of failure and loss.

This act of diving deeply into the feelings we avoid, the feelings we don't necessarily know we have, is our hope of breaking our link in the chain of hurt, suffering, and ineffectiveness. We are human after all. When we avoid the suffering we naturally experience as human beings, we perpetuate it and act against our best interests in relationships.

STRESS IN ACTION:

Montana winters can be harsh. I take every November to February off from training so I can work on other areas of my business. (Such as writing!) I still keep about ten horses on my property, boarded or my own, and I rent out a home on my business property as well. Although I have a small income from this, I still need to have enough money put away to survive the winter until income comes again in spring. One might already see the stress in this situation.

On a cold Montana morning, I received a phone call from my tenants that the well had frozen and they had no water. The temperatures had been in the single to minus digits for a few weeks. As if that wasn't bad enough, I had ten horses on my place with no water! I immediately called well companies. Of course I wasn't the only person with well problems, so they told me they would get to me as soon as they could! Finally I managed to find someone to come out and take a look. My well is in the back yard with a cement cover on the top. The cement was frozen on to the ground and could not be moved. The repairman made a make shift tent and put a heater in it. We hoped the heater could thaw the ground out enough to remove the cover.

That afternoon my truck's "check engine" light went on. Seriously, I thought, this can't be happening! Oh but it was. I took it into the garage in town. They told me they would need the truck for about two days to repair the alternator and put new batteries in the truck. They had nothing in stock so would have to order the parts. The cost would be $1,200.00 I had someone pick me up and take me home only to find the heater wasn't working in my house. It was below10 and I had no heat! So now we have no heat at my home, no water at my facility or the rental property, and my truck was in the shop.

I took a deep breath. I was blessed to have people working hard to help me through this situation. My tenants, who had two small children, were understanding and helped me haul water from another property to the horses. One client picked up three horses and took them home until we fixed the problem. I have a wood stove as a backup heating system in my home, so I was able to keep my house warm.

So, are you thinking big deal, this is nothing compared to what you're facing with a relationship in trouble or a life-threatening illness or maybe even the loss of a loved one. Right? That's my point, if we can't handle the day-to-day stressors how will we ever face the big life stressors that may come our way.

Attitude plays a part in everything we do. I'm not any different, I have my worries and concerns and my life is not perfect. However, I have a choice in how I handle these situations. I choose to look for the positive and to learn from the situation at hand.

The well cover finally thawed out and we discovered the pump switch had frozen in the *off* position. We installed a heater in the well to keep the pump warm. My furnace had a faulty thermostat replaced and my truck was repaired within twenty-four hours. I was thankful I wasn't stranded on the side of the road. Financially this was a setback, in the greater scheme of things, it worked out just fine.

No one said life would be easy; there will always be stress and hardships. Rather than avoiding stressful situations, we need to learn better coping skills. We must learn to have a strong inner sense of self-confidence. How do we do this? First, by not avoiding all stress. Second, become aware of how we handle stressful situations. Third, decide to change and become stronger, more resilient. We should be practicing these skills whenever the opportunity arises. The key here is that these skills are learned. We aren't born with self-assurance. That's good news because we can learn how to handle stress and become stronger physically, mentally, and emotionally.

Stress comes to us in many different areas—money, relationships, business, family, life, death, etc. No one is exempt from pain and hardship. But what if you had the skills to face such adversity and the ability to grow becoming a stronger, happier, and more fulfilled human being? You have everything within you to do just that. Like when I train my horses, I first ask them in small steps. They gain trust and confidence in me, as their handler, and in themselves. My horses have taught me, time and time again, that anything is possible. I challenge you to simply become aware of your thoughts and actions and then, one step at a time, learn to welcome the daily stressors as a time of personal growth and learning. You are stronger than you think!

CHAPTER 30

SUCCESS

The word *success* will mean different things to each person. I find it interesting we all have our own definitions, not only for the word *success,* but each word emphasized throughout this book. Success can come through business, personal achievement, social standings, etc. For some the word *success* equals wealth and prosperity, status, or maybe power. Others may define success by the friendships they have, the work they've done in the community, or possibly through spirituality.

Whatever definition you choose to apply to the word *success,* is the correct answer, because it's your definition. No one else in this world can make that determination but you. Your relationships and life experience all played a role in developing how you see yourself and how you see success in your life.

My definition of success has changed over the years. It will continue to change as I grow as a person. I also believe age plays a part in how we describe success. In my teens success was graduating from high school, landing a good job, and earning a lot of money. In my late twenties success meant owning my home, being self-employed, and having a nice savings account. Again, it's a personal description; a nice savings account will be different for each and every one of us! (I smile as I look back on what success meant to me early on.) In my forties success meant continued personal development, teaching and sharing with others, and creating loving, meaningful relationships.

SUCCESS AND JAG

In 1998 I purchased my horse, Jag, as a four-year-old gelding from a horse dealer. Jag had been born in Sidney, Montana. Sold at auction after auction, not once but three times, before landing in Connecticut at yet another sale barn. (I find it ironic Jag was born in Montana, landed in Connecticut, and then ten years later Montana is home!) When I saw Jag, I knew instantly that he was meant to be my horse. I researched his papers and called his previous owners. They told me Jag was healthy and sound, but showed signs of aggression and was hard to manage. He hadn't been started under saddle because no one connected to him or found him to be "worth" starting.

I honestly never saw any serious issues with this horse. He was four and full of himself, silly, curious, and a bit mischievous. He was also smart and willing and loved to learn. And so began the journey, two lost souls, looking for our fit in the world. I traveled 20,000 miles that first year with Jag. I took him to Colorado for the John Lyons Certification Program. We also traveled and put on demonstrations and clinics and Jag proved to be a perfect gentleman in all situations.

Back then I thought I could save the horse world. I was sure any horse labeled "bad" was simply misunderstood and through kindness and consistency could become a wonderful horse for someone to enjoy. Maybe my youth caused me to have this fairytale idealistic perception, and possibly I was a bit full of myself thinking I was invincible. Much like Jag when he first came into my life. Whatever the case, I began a mission to educate people and make the world a better place for the horse.

Jag taught me: patience, trust, confidence, focus, timing, feel, and he humbled me on more than a few occasions. I watched in awe as this 1,200-pound animal taught me some of the most valuable lessons in life. At the time I had no idea what was going on. I was too wrapped up in my ego to recognize what was happening.

Jag learned all of the pretty maneuvers that so many of us want our horses to perform. He could do flying lead changes, half pass, and canter pirouette. He was patient as I practiced over and over so he'd be able to perform these exercises flawlessly—never a complaint or refusal.

The real work started when we began to work with young horses and "problem horses". To stay safe, I needed to use Jag to pony horses and do some of my work from in the saddle. Although I did my best to always keep Jag and I safe, I admit in those early days poor Jag had his share of kicks, bites, and horses running into him, a few even landed on top of him! He taught me how to position him so that he could best get the job done. Always patient and kind, he seemed to know what each horse needed and he was always honest in whatever situation we were put up against.

While some of the horses I worked with were tough, the owners proved to be even tougher. I would train their horses only to realize the owners were not always willing or sometimes not able to do their part. It was frustrating and exhausting. I knew I had to change what I was doing if I wanted to make a bigger impact.

Jag and I had become a team. We spent long hours together. Jag was my right hand. We'd both grown and matured. We'd been together for almost six years when I decided to take some time off and focus on riding Jag up into the mountains. I was able to take a good hard look at how far Jag and I had come. I believe everything in life happens for a reason. Jag had become my business card. He was why I had a successful equine business. Everywhere people recognized Jag and stopped to pet him. They'd enjoyed watching us at a clinic or demo. I was overwhelmed by the impact he seemed to make on people. Jag is a safe place for most people. He's big, beautiful, and very confident; yet he's kind and gentle and forgiving.

I thought about all the wonderful gifts Jag had given me. He taught me to be patient with horses and with people. He taught me to listen even when I think I know the answer. He taught me to really get to know a horse or a human rather than passing cursory judgment before one gets to know the whole story. He also taught me to get over myself and lighten up. He taught me to have a sense of humor. Because of Jag I met wonderful people, some would become longtime friends while others would come and go, but every one of them gave me a gift of learning, sharing, and growing. Jag taught me courage to move forward in my life and believe in myself. The list goes on and on. Together Jag and I had learned to trust, be confident, and to live life fully.

These were lessons I had to learn in order to go to the next level. On one of the mountain trail rides I realized the best was yet to come. As Jag grazed on a beautiful summer day in the Bitterroot Mountains, I knew we'd outgrown the role of horse trainer. It was time to move forward with a new passion, a new vision. My quest for knowledge began in the areas of mental toughness, performance coaching and leadership lecturing. I knew Jag, and my other horses, would continue to have a vital role in this venture. They are the driving force moving me forward in my riding and in my life.

So do I see myself as successful? You bet! I'm happy, creative, and love life. I enjoy teaching and learning and I'm proud of who I am. I have loving and caring people around me. Although life may throw me a curve ball from time to time, I'm successful in the way I choose to handle the hard times. I have a strong spiritual faith and I've been blessed with a gift to teach and communicate with both horses and humans.

My biggest success was fifteen years ago, when I took that drive to see a horse dealer in Connecticut. I can still see that young, handsome gelding standing in the sale barn aisle. I can still feel my heart skip a beat and feel that overwhelming sense of connection. I can hear myself whispering to the dealer, "I'll take him." And in that moment our lives would never be the same. The journey continues!

CHAPTER 31

TRUST

We think about trust on a logical level and on an emotional level. Everyone has a story about trust, either negative or a positive. Trust, such a simple word, yet it is far from simple. Trust represents the foundation upon which relationships are based whether in the context of a spouse, business, family, or friends. Trust is also internal. Trust is fragile. It's developed through integrity, communication, and action. Trust takes time and history to develop. If trust is compromised, it can take a very long time to repair.

There are three ways to look at trust. One as the person receiving; in other words, you are deciding if someone or something is trustworthy. The second scenario we want to gain someone's trust: are you trustworthy? The third type of trust is learning to trust oneself. This requires self-confidence.

I work very hard at being someone others can trust. I'm honest and sincere. I pride myself that I will not lead someone on in anyway. The joke at my barn? *If you don't want an honest answer then don't ask.* This isn't always an easy task. Being kind and sincere is important when sharing what someone may not want to hear. I know my limitations; therefore when I make a choice—right, wrong or indifferent it'll be okay. After all I trust in myself enough to know I did the best I could and I will learn from it. Learning to trust oneself is important for personal growth and happiness.

TRUST IN ACTION:

When I started out training horses I had very little confidence in my abilities. I had so much to learn and trusting myself was hard. But trusting my horse was even harder. It was scary to think I might hurt my horse or he might hurt me. *What if* played over and over in my mind in the early days.

I was blessed to work with a variety of horses; young horses, older horses, some started some not, problem horses, and show horses. The lessons they taught me have been invaluable in my career. Through these horses I began to grasp the idea of what trust really meant. Horses are amazing creatures; they forgive much more quickly than humans. They taught me that I must be confident, honest, consistent, and, most of all, fair. I also learned that relationships take time and must have a variety of situations that create a reliable history, or pattern.

I hear this almost weekly in my profession: "I have a great horse. I love him so much. He trusts me completely because I spend a huge amount of time brushing him and hanging out with him at the barn. He even knows the sound of my truck when I pull up. My problem is he tends to be spooky on the trail and isn't always easy to load in the trailer and . . ."

This is such a typical complaint. We want so badly to trust and be trusted that we often overlook the obvious. Trust is not built by loving your horse, and feeding him treats. Trust is developed through history and circumstance and a variety of situations that build confidence over time.

A couple spends time together that consists of spending a few hours a day, five days a week, sitting on the couch watching television and visiting a little. A tough situation arises outside of the TV life. The couple love and trusts in the safety of the usual circumstances. But they haven't created the history to trust and believe in that person in other areas. Big problems happen when they don't know how the other party will react. It's the history we develop with people and horses that creates trust and confidence in relationships. Does far-reaching trust develop while sitting on the couch watching television. Maybe? Maybe not? Imagine a fifty-mile drive with someone you barely know, you're on icy roads with the car sliding around. I don't know about you but I would feel uneasy. That uneasiness comes from not knowing the other person's capabilities.

So how do we learn more about trust? Put yourself out there and live, try new things, meet new people, or take a calculated risk. If you get burned, learn from the experience but never stop growing and creating a better and more meaningful life. What a great lesson and gift horses give us if we are able to learn trust with them—why not with everyone?

LILLY

Lilly came for assistance with riding; she owned a little mare but there seemed to be a glitch in their relationship. Lilly had a lot of fear because she was fairly new to riding and she second-guessed herself. She didn't want to take her mare out alone because she was afraid of how this horse might react. Lilly also wanted to learn how to sit the jog, but she did not want to lope, and then added, "I don't have to lope her ever, do I?"

Lilly is quiet and sweet and loves her horses. As we began to work together, I could see that this little mare needed more direction. She was easily agitated if she could not find the answer to what Lilly asked of her. Lilly was trying too hard to be gentle and kind. So this equaled a gray area for horse and rider; and created a lack of trust on both their parts. In any relationship, horse or human, it's important to know where we stand.

This little mare would pin her ears and sull up when Lilly asked her for the jog. Then there was Lilly, close to tears, feeling so badly she could not communicate what seemed like a simple request to her horse. We spent many lessons building good, positive history. We worked on trail obstacles, crossing bridges and poles, and backing around different configurations. Lilly began to recognize when she was sending unclear messages and also recognized when her mare would say *"No, not today!"*

As Lilly became more self-assured, the little mare began to tune in and try harder to find what Lilly wanted. It was an amazing change, one that has taken some time, but I knew Lilly would succeed. Lilly has the desire to learn and do what is right for her horse.

Lilly loped that little mare all around my arena this year with a loose rein, calm and relaxed. Lilly joined a team sorting club (sorting cows in a timed event). She told me at the first sorting that she'd never thought she could do this kind of thing. She felt relaxed and confident and trusted her mare. As I listened, this little mare stood half asleep in the midst of forty plus horses doing their warm ups—her head and neck relaxed, eyes closed, her back foot resting.

This is not the end of the story. It's just the beginning, for the little mare named Journey. She and Lilly are building history and trust one ride at a time!

CHAPTER 32

THE VISION

A vision is your own personal dream, goal, or life passion held deep within your heart. Your vision will begin in your mind and then heart. But if you give it power through words and action, it can become a reality. Remember that a vision is personal. I believe no two people have the same vision; some may appear similar, but I promise your vision will be as unique as you are.

I've asked hundreds of people about the vision for their future. Some willingly describe it with great detail and enthusiasm. Others are reluctant to talk about it. They seem embarrassed to say it out loud. They don't know if others will laugh at them. They're not sure if they're aiming too high or too low. They don't know if their vision is something they can really achieve or are destined to fail.

Some people have no idea how to achieve their dreams. They possess a vague notion there's something they'd like to do someday or someone they'd like to become. But they don't know how to get from here-to-there. If that describes you, then you'll be glad to know there really is hope.

My definition of *vision*: a vision is an inspiring picture of the future that energizes your mind, body, and soul; empowering you to do everything possible to achieve it. A vision worth pursuing is a picture and blueprint of a person's purpose and potential.

MY VISION

You could call me a dreamer. From the time I was old enough to ride on the school bus I began to envision myself traveling, riding horses, training horses, and teaching. One of my first memories of this (I was too young to know I had a vision!) was at eight years old. I pressed my forehead against the school bus window and pictured myself galloping alongside the bus through pastures and over the golf course greens. I'd ride like the wind. I spent countless hours talking into a tape recorder about horse training. I wanted to write a book and teach people about horses. My dad gave me a two-year-old filly, Cherry, and I was determined to train her myself. I was eight! When I hit high school, I journaled everything because I could see myself writing a book. In fact my mother, Aunt Margaret, and Grandmother loved to read my essays. They often told me someday I would publish a book.

In my twenties I began putting on little demonstrations on horse training for anyone who would watch and listen. I had a vision of owning a well-bred paint horse, and the vision of a log home with the long gravel driveway. When I was thirty-eight, the log home vision became a reality.

Almost anything I've envisioned, and felt passionate about, has become my reality. I'm living my dream, training horses and people, writing, lecturing, and developing programs that encourage people to live their passion. I share this with you because I believe, with all my heart, you can achieve anything you desire no matter how big or small.

WHAT DO YOU HAVE IN MIND

Having a vision is a valuable commodity. Vision propels us forward. Vision gives us energy. Vision makes us enthusiastic. Everyone ought to have a vision. But what if you're not sure whether you have a vision to pursue?

I've learned over the last few years to take the ego away and have patience. Do what you want—don't let anyone tell you to do a version of what you want. Hold on tight to your vision and then, wait it out. Even if it takes *forever*. Even if you don't blow up in two seconds as the biggest, world-dominating super star, stick to it. You will grow incrementally.

Always remember there are two kinds of people in this world—the realist and the visionary. The realists know where they're going. The visionaries have already been there!

At my clinics and workshops we talk about what might spark enthusiasm in someone. Think about a good herding dog. Pen him up and he will lie around the yard all day, unmotivated and with little enthusiasm. He just drags through his day. However when his owner gets home, opens up the bed of that pickup truck, and the dog realizes he's about to go to work bringing in the livestock, that dog comes alive! He jumps and barks running around with excitement. A definite night and day difference. Why? Because herding dogs are wired that way. They have a natural passion and a natural excitement about herding. They don't have to work themselves up to be happy. They don't say, "Well, maybe if I go listen to a motivational speaker or maybe if I read something that inspires me . . ." then maybe I'll feel like herding. No, when those dogs go out to work they're sincerely excited about it. They have the desire in their heart. It's instinctual.

When we do what we are called to do, when we follow our heart, we become naturally excited. We may not jump up and down every day, but there is a peace in our heart knowing we're doing what we were born to do. Sometimes going down one path leads to an entirely different place, one we never saw coming. Stay flexible as long as it feels right and inspires you. Life is about the lessons we learn. Change is part of those lessons. I've fought change from time to time, but when I look back the change was always for the better.

Sometimes success doesn't come quickly or easily. Sometimes we must learn the hard way. We may not even feel headed in the right direction. We can't be great at everything, but there is something that makes each of us feel full and alive. I can't play a guitar (and I really want to!) but I can start a colt and keep him calm and quiet with little effort.

As a kid I spent countless hours in the barn. Sometimes I'd just crawl all over my horse, sleeping on his back while he grazed in the pasture. My summers were filled with swimming with my horses, riding the trails, and cleaning stalls. I remember more than once meeting my grandmother for lunch. I can still see her wrinkle up her nose and say, "Kathryn, did you just come from the barn?" Grandma wasn't a horse enthusiast. To her I always smelled like a horse and wore clothes that were less than suitable for a young lady. I never noticed either the smell or the clothes. To me I looked cool. Who wouldn't love the smell of a horse! I was happy. The hours of my childhood simply passed by as if they were minutes.

Your vision will be determined by what excites you. A picture held in your mind that makes you happy and fills you with energy. Often our visions are linked to something we loved to do as a child. We get caught up in the responsibilities of adult life and we forget to dream. What are you passionate about? What is your vision for your future?

CHAPTER 33

MY WISH

I hope this is the beginning of a wonderful experience for you and a chance to reflect on your own stories with meaningful words like: Adaptability, Creativity, Passion, Strategy, and Success. Words are powerful and so are you.

One of my favorite movies is *Chariots of Fire*. In this film Eric Liddell is a gifted runner whose dream is to compete in the Olympics. He knows God has given him the gift of running. In one of the classic lines from the movie, Liddell says, "When I run, I feel God's pleasure." He meant when we do what we're called to do, when we using our gifts and talents, when we're pursuing destiny, God smiles down on us. That's how I feel about teaching and training: when I teach, when I ride, when I write—I feel God's pleasure.

When I first started teaching years ago I thought it was all about training. How wrong I was! I've come to realize it's all about people; people learning about who they are and about life. Horse and rider become a team. From that gift the human grows and shares their life experience. Possibly they may learn what it really means to be human. No one thing, no one cue you teach your horse is ever just about that one cue. It will affect and flow over to many other areas in your horses training. This is true for everything in life. No one thing, not one experience is just about that one moment. It will flow over and allow us to grow if we are willing to listen and learn from it.

An old Cherokee tale tells of a grandfather teaching life principles to his grandson. The wise old Cherokee said, "Son, on the inside of every person a battle is raging between two wolves. One wolf is evil. It's angry, jealous, unforgiving, proud, and lazy. The other wolf is good. It's filled with love, kindness, humility, and self-control. These two wolves are constantly fighting."

The little boy thought about this and said, "Grandfather, which wolf is going to win?"

The grandfather smiled and said, "Which ever one you nurture."

You were never created to be average. You were never created to reach a certain level and plateau. You were created to excel. There is no limit to how high you can go in life. There is no limit to what you can accomplish, if you believe in yourself and keep learning and stretching to the next level. I hope you will give birth to your dreams and the desires you hold in your heart.

Words are powerful, I want to say thank you for taking the time to read *"Life According to Jag."*